This book m
Replacement cost wi

Vous devez ret
Le coût de rer
livre n est pas retourné.

MW00981339

RETURN BY/DATE DE RETOUR		

COMOX MILITARY FAMILY
RESOURCE CENTRE
CANADIAN FORCES BASE COMOX
Box 310, LAZO, B.C. V0R 2K0

FOR THOSE
LEFT BEHIND

A guide for loved ones who are facing a deployment

Cherisa Jerez

First published by AuthorHouse 7/16/2009

ISBN-13: 978-1491018217
ISBN-10: 1491018216

This book is printed on acid free paper

U.S. Air Force photo on cover by Tech. Sgt. Erik Gudmundson.

This book is dedicated to my Lord and Savior for the divine inspiration and the never ending partnership and to my loving husband. Thank you for your sacrifice, your bravery, and your willingness to proudly defend the freedom of the greatest country in the world.

Acknowledgments

It's important to me to first and foremost, thank my Father God for his divine inspiration, blessing, and protection as I began to form the idea for this book sitting in my HMMWV at the motor pool in Fort Bliss, Texas. Thank you Father. Not only for your call in my life but also for the strength to finish what we started together.

I also have to thank my husband for choosing to say yes with bravery and dignity when duty called. I know it wasn't easy and it was a time we will never forget, but I thank you for your patience and push to finish the book.

Finally, I must thank the following soldiers: SGT Heather Morrill, SPC Jessica Shaffer, and SPC Christopher Colin. Thank you so much for your time, your honesty, and your willingness to share your experience with the rest of us. Your service is forever remembered.

Contents

Foreword by
CPT Alberto M. Jerez

Spending fifteen months in a combat zone away from my wife and children was probably the most challenging time in my life. I had just started a life with the love of my life, when a few weeks after our wedding I found myself at the National Training Center in California getting ready to deploy to Mosul, Iraq.

Throughout all the preparation for my deployment I kept wondering how I was going to deal with this separation. I thought about the mind games I would play with myself to make it through the deployment without going crazy. But little did I know that as difficult as this deployment would be on me, it would be even worse for those I was leaving behind—my family, especially my wife.

On October 31, 2007, I arrived in Kuwait and began to prepare for my year-long tour in a foreign country. As I set foot on the ground, I remember telling myself, "One down, three hundred and sixty-four to go."

I was so preoccupied with getting back to my family so that I could kiss my daughter goodnight and rub my wife's belly and sing to my unborn child that I never took the time to think how they were doing. I figured everything was fine back in the United States. I was the one who was away, and when the news broke out, "All units have been extended to fifteen months," I was the only one who had to deal with that too. Wasn't I?

I knew my wife was a strong, independent woman who knew how to take care of things. Why would I worry about her? Her life was great! She, of course, saw it in a different light.

She was recently married, starting a new job, taking care of a four-year-old girl, attending graduate school, pregnant, and alone. Looking at her situation one would think, "Wow, she had her hands full!" and while that was true, the mental strain she had to endure was far worse than the physical effort she put forth to keep our family going.

How was she going to do it? How was she going to deal with it all and manage to not go crazy?

You will find your answer in the pages of this book. It will take you through one of the toughest times in our journey through life. It will expose the good, the bad, and the ugly of such hardship. If you have already gone through a similar situation, then you will be able to relate. If you are getting ready to send your loved one away to war, then hopefully this book will help you prepare for the challenges ahead and give some guidance to go the "distance" in your relationships.

Good luck!

Introduction

The Lord bless you my daughter ... (Ruth 3:10).
Now don't worry about a thing, my daughter...
(Ruth 3:11).

I had been tossing around the idea of this book for nine months or so. It became clear to me that this would be something I wanted to do when I was faced with the reality that a very special man in my life had been called to serve his country. My husband, who had proudly served in the United States Army for nine years, was now on orders to face his very first deployment in Iraq.

I can't even begin to imagine what was going through his mind as he prepared to leave a brand-new bride, who was expecting their first child, to travel around the globe and fight for the enduring freedom of the world; yet I clearly remember what was going through mine. And so began the budding development of this book. I realized that I had just joined a very large and often humbly silent group of spouses and loved ones left behind to continue with their lives with an essential piece of that life missing.

My hopes with this book are not to provide any new profound answers as to what it takes to make this easier. Unfortunately, I don't really have those. My intention is simply to provide understanding and support. My desire is simply to touch the hearts and souls of family members and loved ones everywhere who have had to face the reality of saying goodbye to someone they love. My desire is to offer a different perspective, for not only do I understand how it feels to be the one, who is left behind, but I too am a soldier, and I am clearly able to grasp the call to duty, the love of country, and the freedoms we defend.

At the end of each chapter, beginning with chapter 2, there are two areas dedicated to my readers. One is designed as a journal entry. I am giving you the first line of the journal entry in hopes that I may inspire some thoughts and ideas for you. Oftentimes for many people there is healing and understanding when they are able to see their thoughts and feelings on paper. This can also be used as a point of reference throughout the book as you go back and see where you were and take pride in where you're going on this emotional and life-changing journey.

I've also included the points to ponder section. This is an area of the book solely dedicated to encouragement and understanding for you, the reader. It's a reflection of the things I faced in that chapter and the summary to it all. I hope that it gives you a better perspective on things as you may see them from an entirely different approach.

My goal is that these two sections help to make this book not only a comfort, but also a tool for those faced with the responsibility and gift of loving someone who has been called to greatness and service.

My personal approach to this entire experience has been to rely on the strengths of the Lord I serve and the scriptures that I believe he uses to communicate with me. At the beginning of each chapter I offer the words of wisdom from a pretty verifiable source through scripture to serve as my guide as I journey through one of the most difficult, life changing, trying, and yet gratifying times in my life. Welcome to my journey.

Chapter 1

Breaking the News—My Story

But despite all this, I will not utterly reject or despise them while they are in exile in the land of their enemies. I will not cancel my covenant with them by wiping them out. I, the Lord, am their God. (Lev. 26:44).

We can make our plans, but the Lord determines our steps. (Prov. 16:9).

I joined the United States Army to become an officer during a time of war. In doing so I understood the potentials of war I was facing. Almost all recruits at that time were being trained and shipped off to fight the war on terror. I must admit, though, having recently graduated with a degree in accounting, there was a big part of me that was hoping I'd land a position as a finance officer, travel to some post in the United States, and handle any financial related issues behind a desk. This turned out to be hardly the case.

Instead I became a signal officer, joining the same group of soldiers that are often the first in the fight setting up communications and the last to leave as they wait for the green light to take those same communications down. It was hardly what I would call a desk job. I spent nine months learning infantry type battlefield tactics and warrior tasks and drills. Needless to say, by the time my training was complete I was physically and mentally prepared to go to war and head into battle.

I met my husband during this time. He was an engineer officer in the army and on orders to become a member of a unit deploying to Iraq. After a whirlwind romance, he signed in to the unit two days after we were married. One day later we learned we were expecting a child. Things were happening for us fast and furiously, and neither one of us was coming up for air. We were merely riding the wave, hanging on for dear life, and hoping for the best.

Looking back one year later I can now reflect on the inner complexity of that time for me. I was very torn between some of the greatest events of my life coming together at the same time. I had just married the love of my life, I was expecting his child in the spring, and yet I was facing some major professional sacrifices. Up until I had discovered the pregnancy, I had built visions of us deploying together, living the adventure, and fighting this war side by side. Those visions were now overshadowed by home-binding, life-altering events.

Rather than go and fight the war on terror and lead as I had been trained, I had to face entering my first army assignment as a pregnant soldier. This posed some unexpected challenges both physically and emotionally. It was also a thrust into a completely new and unknown world. Where I had initially envisioned myself deployed on some remote installation in Iraq, I was now the pregnant wife of a soldier, left behind while he went to honor his duty to our great country. I was forced to support him and wait at home. For the first time in my life I truly understood the great sacrifice that was to be made and the even greater sacrifice were he not to return.

I was given four months to prepare myself for the time that he would be deployed, and I would then be left alone to maintain a job, attend graduate school, raise my two other children, and prepare for the final trimester of my pregnancy and the birth of our child. Needless to say, I was overwhelmed and extremely afraid and definitely not prepared.

Four months hardly seemed like enough time, and yet I was grateful, as I had seen other families that were only given a couple of weeks to prepare. Looking back, I don't think there is a right amount of time to prepare for this type of departure—one that could be the very last time you see your service member. I've since learned that all you can do is move forward and get your things in order. The rest has to come from your own personal strength and will in order to survive this experience.

Some people out there may think that I am the oddity in the population, some overextended type-A personality taking on more than humanly possible. But contrary to popular belief in today's society, I am not the oddity at all. In fact, I seem to represent this growing population of family members, loved ones, and close friends waiting for their loved one who is deployed for a year or more at a time.

Men and women alike are facing a future of up to fifteen months where they are required to hold down full-time jobs, attend school to further their education, care for two, three, sometimes four or more young children, and be the support system for their spouse.

It is no wonder the divorce rate is as high as it is! We have a group of strong, dedicated men and women who go above and beyond to do their part for the freedoms of this country, and instead of support and recognition, they are simply faced with a constant stream of negative press and news that they are facing the possibilities of even longer deployments and separations from their family.

The realization of this book was never an opportunity to exploit a hot topic. I did the research and searched for a guidebook, a companion through the pages, something that would tell me I wasn't alone. Throughout all my searching I simply realized that there isn't much literature out there for those left behind, and as new member of this growing population, I would like to give my peace offering. This is a book that will relate to many, understand those who are away, and provide the leverage to reach out and say it's all okay. There is no wrong or right way to handle this. It's never easy, and for those that make it seem as though it is … they're totally lying!

Finally, I've written this book for all of those waiting loved ones who feel completely alone. Not only are there thousands of people in your same situation who are more than willing to reach out, but there is someone way up in the heavens who is quietly whispering to your heart that no matter how you may feel, you are never alone. I thank the Lord above that I may be a tool to show so many others in this world that this journey is not easy, but it doesn't have to be accomplished on your own. There is help, and there is support. All you have to do is turn the page or close your eyes and pray. I wish you the best of luck on your journey. Fathers, daughters, husbands, wives, sons, cousins, and friends alike, welcome to the team of those left behind.

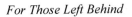

For Those Left Behind

Chapter 2
Denial

So don't worry about tomorrow, for tomorrow will bring its own worries. Today's trouble is enough for today. (Matt. 6:34).

I must consider myself one of the lucky ones. I had at least four months to get ready for this. There are units in the today's military that are often told only a few weeks or even days before deployment that they are leaving. Don't get me wrong—those types of units prepare the service member for the realities they continually face. Training is intense, equipment is constantly monitored, and readiness is the number one priority, but how do you really prepare your significant other and your children for such an event? How do you sit an innocent three year old down on the couch and say any time now Daddy may have to go away for a long time and so we must be ready? How do you comfort an eighteen-month-old child who is crying for her mother, knowing that she is on a plane to Kuwait fulfilling her duties to her country and the brothers and sisters in arms to her left and right?

It isn't easy. Initially there is denial and lots of it, especially for the first timer. I was a first timer. I had never experienced having to let go of someone you love, praying that he would come home safely, fearing that he might not. I honestly spent the four months I had to wait before his unit deployed in total denial. I assured myself that somehow it was all going to change. At the very last minute the unit's mission would be canceled, their orders terminated. Somehow, some way, God would intervene and keep my husband home with me.

Fortunately for him, the unit and its leaders accepted the reality of their situation immediately and quickly began preparing for the yearlong deployment to the Middle East. Appointments were scheduled, injections were issued, and forms were updated to include the soldier's last will and testament and their life insurance plans in case they were killed in combat.

The training intensified, and the speeches and the forums began informing the involved spouses of some of the things they would be facing. Like a devoted and caring spouse, I attended these briefings, but in my mind I was merely going through the motions. There was no way my husband was leaving. I, too, was in the army; I knew how things changed. They changed all the time. Surely my guardian angel was planning to intervene and keep my family together. I was not willing to accept my fate as an expectant mother having to face the final and most difficult trimester of my pregnancy alone. Things were going to change; the unit was not going to deploy. I had convinced myself of that, and in essence protected my heart with the reassurance that this was all procedural and the news would change.

The news never changed. October 30th did roll around. His bags were packed in the living room. His bags were loaded in our truck. We drove to the army post and walked into a gymnasium full of families. Oddly, I remember all the balloons more than anything else that day.

There were red, white, and blue balloons taped to the bleachers all around us. I must commend the family oriented organizations for the efforts put into these types of events. The smell of hamburgers and hotdogs wafted in the air, upbeat music played in the background. The balloons were used to remind us all of the patriotic mantra that envelops the military member's spirit. They represented the colors of our great nation and reminded us that not only are many of these men and women mothers and fathers, sisters and brothers, but they are the hopes of many great nations in the world and the great resource of one nation in particular. At that very moment the average parents, siblings, sons, and daughters put on their military uniform, secured their gear, and prepared themselves to become a part of something great.

The atmosphere in the gymnasium that day was intense. You could feel the spouses' grief in the air mixed with the energy of the children running around loaded up on cotton candy and lollipops. I watched the expressions of duty and responsibility on the chaplains' faces as their eyes scanned the room. Their lips barely parted in soft spoken prayer for the soldiers and their families, both for those present in that room and for those who didn't have the courage to make it. Most importantly, I watched the soldiers themselves.

It was odd, the mixture of expressions on their faces; odd, the mixture of emotions in my heart. To be completely honest, one part of me was jealous. The men and women leaving on the plane that day were fulfilling their job. They were doing what they had signed up to do. The soldier in me could feel the pride of that, to finally go out there and do what the army had trained you to do.

That room was full of emotions that morning. There was fear and excitement all at the same time. It was strange how out of all the things I thought I would feel and all the things I knew I would feel, I was impacted most by an unexpected emotion— envy. I was envious that my husband was being given the chance to go out there and fight the war on terror. I was envious of the opportunity he was being given to make a difference to a people we believed needed our assistance. I was envious of his chance to leave a soldier and return a hero, having experienced the real war and not what is told to you through PowerPoint presentations. And that was when it hit me. What was all that opportunity worth to me if he didn't come back at all?

Then the denial returned.

I remember continuously staring at the exit of the gymnasium. Every ten minutes or so I would turn my head toward the door waiting for someone to call the room to attention as some three-star general walked in and apologized for the inconvenience. I waited for him to apologize and inform everyone that the unit would not be deploying after all. It's silly I know, the hopeless dreams of a young woman in love, but on that day they were as real to me as the soldiers standing in line in front of me turning in their paperwork and picking up their flight itineraries.

I recall being very moved by one female soldier in particular. She was standing in line with her family waiting her turn for her fate to be sealed. She was holding her infant daughter in her arms. The baby didn't look more than three months old. However, I was familiar with army policy, which requires that a newborn be four months old before the mother is once again deployable, and it occurred to me that she had probably just made the cutoff mark. I watched with admiration as this young woman handed her baby to its father and fixed her gaze forward in acceptance and pride. Many in the room that day probably didn't grasp the level of sacrifice this young mother had just made for her country, but I did. I rubbed my own belly as I watched her. I felt for the life growing inside me, and I was thankful for the courage of thousands of men and women fighting this war every day. I had seen selflessness at its best. At minimum it was a sacrifice of time between a mother and her infant child; at most this could cost her life.

We were there maybe an hour or two at most. I sat beside my husband with a million thoughts racing through my mind. Finally, they announced it was time. The soldiers were being transported to the airfield, and the families would have to say their goodbyes. I walked my husband down the bleachers, and wanting to protect him from the heartbreak of a long goodbye, I gave him a kiss and a hug, wished him luck, and left.

I didn't look back. I couldn't or I knew I wouldn't have been able to leave. I walked quickly toward our car, passing a group of women hugging one another and crying in great bursts of sorrow. I knew how they felt. I knew more than longing there was fear—the fear that it may have been the last time they would ever see their loved one again.

The most difficult part of that day was the drive home. I closed the car door, and felt the silence and the emptiness. I turned the ignition, and the car filled up with sound from the radio, but I shut the radio off because the music felt like an invasion of my anguish. I drove home, and the denial had fled. I realized then that he was gone, that he wasn't going to be home that night and many nights thereafter. For the next year I was on my own and in the midst of it all, and in three more months I was going to give birth to our baby. And so it began …

Journal Entry

1.   My soldier left today, and I feel …

_____

_____

_____

_____

_____

_____

_____

_____

_____

_____

_____

_____

_____

_____

Point to Ponder

This will get easier with time. You may feel overwhelmed today, but you must remember that time never stops. This year will go very quickly, and there's a plan that the Lord has just begun in your life. Be excited!

Chapter 3

The Initial Shock

Dear brothers and sisters, whenever trouble comes your way, let it be an opportunity for joy. For when your faith is tested, your endurance has a chance to grow. So let it grow, for when your endurance is fully developed, you will be strong in character and ready for anything. (James 1:2–4).

Turning a new leaf is always easier said than done. That doesn't necessarily mean it can't be done; it just means it's never as easy as they say. The first night I spent alone I was afraid. I was afraid of all the things I would bear alone. I was afraid of having our baby alone. I was afraid of having to maintain our home alone, afraid of the silent nights where this is no conversation and no one to talk to. It was a new beginning for me, and in the beginning I was afraid.

This would begin my journey and my new walk with God. There is no question in my mind that the

Lord does not teach us through pain or anguish. Our God is a God of love who is always reaching out to protect his people, but I do believe that when you are receptive to it, the Lord will do great things in your life and set the conditions to build an intimate relationship with you. These were my conditions, and it wasn't long before I came to realize that my worries at that time were misconstrued. I had no need to fear. The Lord had not left me, and I was not alone. On the contrary, he was closer to me than ever, silently assuring me I needed to cast my cares on him.

However, the first night was saturated with anxiety. The burdens of everyday life seemed to multiply over night. Paying the bills, driving the children to daycare, performing at work, going to school one night a week, even having to cook dinner and wash the dishes—all of these tasks combined seemed inconceivable for one woman alone. And then there was the silence. The silence was suffocating.

My two daughters were eleven and four years old when my husband first deployed, and they already had a sense that perhaps their mommy needed to be alone to regroup and mourn. During the drive home I was battling between the realizations of my situation and the need to console and protect my children. The attempted efforts to let them know I was okay and he would be home soon hung in the air as we entered our home in virtual silence. The girls headed up to their rooms to play. I went to my room to mourn. The strength children possess still astounds me every day. Their resilience is remarkable.

Upon entering our bedroom I was forced with the realization that I could still smell his cologne in the air. I could feel the footprints in the carpet where he had stood. I stared at the sheets were we had lain together in one another's arms that morning trying to block out the veracity of our immediate future. It was true there was no turning back; he was on a plane heading to the other side of the world. Just as we were beginning a new life and a new family, he was being taken away. I loved this man more that day for his courage then I had ever loved him before. Yet I was mourning his departure. Perception is everything. Looking back, one year really isn't that long a time in comparison to a lifetime together. However, when you're staring at that year from day one, it seems endless and overwhelming.

The First Phone Call

My husband deployed to Iraq on a sunny Monday morning in October. I didn't hear from him again until Wednesday afternoon. It was a brief phone call, and he sounded exhausted. He had little time to talk. Being a service member myself, I could clearly envision the lines that must be forming behind him filled with husbands and wives, mothers and fathers, and brothers and sisters also anxious to speak to their loved ones. I knew I didn't have much time, and yet I had so much to say. I wanted so badly to pour my heart out. I wanted to tell him that I was lonely and afraid. I wanted to tell him that I couldn't put my hands around this idea of living the next twelve months without him. I wanted to scream into the phone that he needed to come back home and be there to hold my hand in the delivery room during the birth of his baby girl. Instead I was silent and agreeable.

I had a greater need to be supportive of my husband. Looking back I understand that this was a benefit of my military training and experience. I had an idea of what it was like for him. The pressures, the concerns, the thoughts—I could relate to it all from a smaller perspective. Looking back on a time when I had to make that first phone call from basic training, I could remember the fear of the unknown and the sorrow that accompanied the realization that I had left my family and I was on my own. And so instead of unloading everything that I was going through, I empathized with him and was able to offer him what he needed.

Many spouses out there don't understand this concept. Initially they are afraid and their fears and anxieties consume everything else. They have no understanding of what it's like for the soldier. It is difficult to look beyond the responsibility and challenges of what is going on around you and place yourself thousands of miles away in a foreign country around people you may not know very well and will be forced to live with for the next year of your life. And so without realizing it, oftentimes our good intentions and need for support and reassurance turn into a sobbing spouse on the phone begging the soldier to come back home, telling them they can't make it, that it's just too hard.

In turn you have soldiers who hang up that same phone in sadness and disbelief. Rather than having peace that all is taken care of, they are now worrying about the family at home. Is he/she going to be able to make it? Will he/she wait for me? Will the bills get paid on time? The pressures of everything going on around them and the newfound realities of not being there for their family can be extremely overwhelming. From day one we have the power of those left behind to set our soldier up for success. Ultimately we must make that choice the sends them to war focused and ready or preoccupied, distracted, and distressed.

The Flip Side

Oftentimes there is a great sense of duty that calls thousands of great men and women to serve their country in war. Th at same characteristic that drives a soldier to greatness can also spill into other areas of his or her life. My soldier fell into this category. He is very in touch with his sense of duty, especially to his family. Sometimes this need to ensure that all things on the home front are being taken care of can be misinterpreted as a lack of concern for the emotional wellbeing of the spouse.

I fell into this category. That first phone call I tried to be strong for my soldier. I wanted him to know that I was okay, that I had a handle on everything going on. It wasn't until I hung up the phone in tears that I realized that I wasn't okay. I needed his reassurance. I needed to hear how much he was missing me and how much he wished none of this was going on. I didn't want to hear any excitement or anticipation in his voice; selfishly, I wanted to hear the sorrow in his voice that I was feeling in my heart.

I realize now the unfairness of that, but at that time I was torn apart by that first phone call. My expectations of a Hollywood-level phone call where we both declared our undying love and devotion was circumvented by his practicality and need to ensure that all last-minute plans were taken care of. We discussed the bills, the bank accounts, the power of attorney, the children, and the fact that he had arrived safely. I was devastated. I hung up the phone feeling as though I had just placed a business call to my financial advisor. I was resentful at the lack of emotion. And rather than take comfort in his good intentions to provide for and protect his family, I focused on what was not being said.

Words of Advice

Friends, family, fellow spouses, don't make that same mistake. If you're reading this book before your soldier has deployed, remember this: your soldier is about to face the next twelve to fifteen months in solitude from his or her family and all that he or she knows. This single act of deploying to war requires one of the greatest acts of commitment and bravery that you will ever see.

God has given you a gift by including you as a part of something this great. And ultimately that same individual who is showing exemplary commitment to a call of duty is the same person who has committed to you. Find faith and happiness in that. Take comfort that you are being provided and cared for. Don't make the mistake that I did and focus on the words. Instead, search your heart and look on the other side of that phone. Look all the way on the other side of the world, where your loved one is fighting the sense of powerlessness. Your loved one's greatest fear is that he or she forgot to take care of something that will help to make your life better.

I titled this chapter the initial shock because that is exactly what it is—shock. We all handle shock differently. Some of us panic, others detach; some throw themselves into mundane little tasks and continue throughout the situation in denial. All of these reactions and feelings are valid and real. The important thing to remember is acknowledgment.

Acknowledge how you are handling the initial shock. Use this book as a tool to sort out your thoughts and feelings. Be ready to discuss this with your loved one when you get that first phone call. It may be fears and concerns, or it may be words of encouragement and gratitude for their sacrifice. Ultimately what is most important is that you don't make the biggest mistake possible by saying nothing at all.

Journal Entry

It's all finally happening. My soldier is gone and I really want to say that …

_____

_____

_____

_____

_____

_____

_____

_____

Point to Ponder

Your soldier has given one of the greatest gifts he or she could ever give. He or she has given him or herself up for the call of service and duty to serve the people of this great country and fight for our enduring freedom. Remember that there are so many last-minute details going through your loved one's mind on that trip to the other side of the world. Comfort your soldier. Let him or her know that he or she is already loved and missed and be receptive to how he or she handled the initial shock.

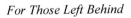

For Those Left Behind

Chapter 4

Reflection, Reminiscing & Regret

*Turn to me and have mercy on me, for I am
alone and in deep distress. My problems go from
bad to worst; Oh save me from them all! Feel my
pain and see my trouble. Forgive all my sins.
(Ps. 25:16–18).*

This is the breaking point. This is the one effect
of a deployment that I can virtually guarantee every
individual person close to a deployed soldier will go
through at least once during the deployment. For
most of us it happens at the very beginning; for
others it may take a little bit longer. And for those
very unfortunate souls, it can occur at a point where
it's too late.

I believe this to be one of the most important
chapters in the book. Not only does it begin to occur
almost immediately, but reflection, reminiscing, and

regret oriented thoughts can take over the entire time if you're not careful. These three areas can be some of the greatest tools for growth and intimacy or the final say on disappointment, destruction, and disintegration of the relationship between you and your soldier. For some people out there, if they are not careful regret can be emotionally suffocating and kill the human spirit as quickly as it kills the individual.

I remember a lot of people telling me that absence makes the heart grow fonder. What does that mean exactly? Does it mean that I miss my soldier simply because he or she's not around? Does it mean that my love has grown the minute he or she boarded the plane and I was left to face the world as I know it on my own? Absence makes the heart grow fonder. It's a powerful statement, but it can mean many different interpretations. It can mean what you make it mean. You're probably reading this and thinking, "I don't understand."

Let me help clarify. Our hearts were affected the moment we knew our soldier would have to leave. Had you not been affected you would not be reading this book right now. For some the initial reaction may have been surprise and for some that surprise in turn may have become relief. Let me assure you that feeling relieved is natural. There is nothing to feel guilty about. If a current situation, marriage, or friendship isn't turning out the way you had intended and your days are filled with constant fighting and stress, then the thought of a "break" from the situation can be comforting. I realize that the events leading up to the break are pretty severe, but for many of those left behind they have no concept of what the soldier is about to experience or face, so it's easy to look at the short term aspect of their own situations. First, things are not working out very well, and second, your soldier will be well taken care of by his or her employer and you will get a much-needed break.

Understanding that what you're feeling is normal is the first step. The second step is to begin to analyze what is going wrong or really well in the relationship. Make the most of your separation; make it count for you as much as it does for the soldiers. They are the soldiers, and they know what they have to do. They have been trained. They have a job to do. They are called to duty. They are about to experience what being a soldier in the U.S. military is really all about. The soldier has a sense of purpose.

What Are You Feeling?

Oftentimes the spouse or loved one is missing that same sense of purpose. You may feel as though you're simply along for the ride. You may believe that loving a soldier means that you completely give up the sense of control in your life. The soldier belongs to the military first and to you second.

27

Try to combat this method of thinking. Your soldier is still your loved one first and foremost. The military has merely called on your loved one to protect and serve those who fight beside him or her to his or her right and left. Give yourself the same sense of purpose. Utilize this time of separation as a time of reflection to rectify the misgivings and battles in your relationship. If the relationship is on high ground, use this time to continue to uplift and nurture a good thing.

For those who are guiltily feeling relieved, admit the relief and rebuke the guilt. It isn't necessary to carry an extra burden on your back. There's relief for a reason. Something in the relationship between you and your soldier needs to be worked on. It may be something as small as a monopoly of the TV that you no longer have to face or a much deeper-rooted issue, such as a lack of communication. Either way, there is a specific issue relating to this sense of relief. You have now been given nothing but time to search your soul and figure it out.

Analyze the Relationship

Understand that initially the things going wrong may be clear, but as time passes, they will get fuzzier. Time has been described as a healer of all wounds. Actually, all that means is that oftentimes, especially during periods of long separation, it is very easy to focus on all the great qualities and lose touch with one's relationship flaws and what caused that initial sense of relief in the first place.

Your soldier is going to have so many different things running through his or her mind as he or she faces a long term deployment and all that it entails, but his or her sense of purpose is fairly clear. You, on the other hand, may not have this clear vision, and this separation is the ideal time to really figure it all out. My own recommendation is that you immediately remove the rose-colored glasses and look at your situation for what it is. If it's great, it's great, but if it's not, then now more than ever is the time to look back, analyze it, and fix it.

I am not by any means implying that a soldier is blameless or unnecessary in the correction of problems and concerns in a relationship. I am merely talking about opportunity. This may be a first-time opportunity that you will have some "me" time. This is time to dedicate solely to yourself and how you really feel about this relationship and the direction its heading. Take advantage of it. Let me use the following illustration to really drive home my point.

Let's consider Jane Smith. Jane Smith is married to SSG Smith. She is helping him pack his duffel bag in preparation for an extended fourteen-month deployment to Baghdad, Iraq. They have known about the deployment for the last forty-five days and have been consistently arguing ever since. They have argued about everything from her current circle of friends to the times she will leave the house in the morning to drop off the children. The latest argument consists of whether or not she even cares that he's leaving because she's been behaving so distantly since finding out. That night their situation escalated with him discovering that she had put in a request to work more hours the week before he deployed. Their fight ends with the two of them yelling at the top of their lungs and he storms off to the couch to sleep.

Jane and SSG Smith have been married for eighteen months and now at twenty-two years old, she is the mother of a five year old boy from a previous relationship and an infant baby girl. She works full time at the commissary on post stocking groceries and takes classes one night a week to earn her college degree. She doesn't understand why the fighting has gotten so bad between the two of them, and she feels resentful that he has no compassion for the situation she's about to face. In her mind he's leaving her alone and she's afraid.

SSG Smith deploys with his unit the very next morning, and the situation between the two of them is tense. He is angry with his wife for not having more compassion for his situation and comforting him through his fear and frustration at having to leave. He believes that he's in the position he's in so that he may be able to provide for her and the children, and deep down inside he's angry that she doesn't seem very crushed about his leaving. He wonders if she's going to miss him at all.

Trying to put a brave front for her husband, Jane comes across detached and aloof. Inside she's angry and confused and mostly afraid but doesn't know how to express this to him. Jane also wants to be fair and be strong for her soldier so that he won't worry about her. He leaves that morning with a quick hug and very few words. The void between them is great, and Jane feels guilty at the sense of relief she feels as she walks away. In her mind the fighting is over and she can focus on her daily duties and caring for her children.

Does this sound strangely familiar? Was this your story or something pretty close to it? What happens when a week later "Jane" is so wrapped up in missing her husband that she can't remember any of the issues they faced before he left? Nothing gets resolved, that's what happens. Instead the focus is quickly shifted to all the odds and ends, all of the little details. Jane has now lost touch with some very real coping issues in her marriage, but her unwillingness to reflect and deal with them from the very beginning can have some very serious consequences and will only postpone the inevitable.

Tips for Immediate Reflection

1. Write down a list of what went wrong. Include specific subjects of arguments and how they made you feel.

2. Pray for peace and wisdom before you approach these subjects to your loved one, and ask the Lord to open his or her heart and be receptive.

3. Next to each subject on your list identify if it was the actual issue that was bothering you or something bigger. For example, for Jane Smith the arguments about her circle of friends probably had little to do with how he felt about her friends and more to do with his desire to hear her say that she would make him priority number one in her life and he could not be replaced while he's gone.

Reminiscing

I can't begin to describe the value and importance of this. Reminiscing can be a double-edged sword. It can distort the reality if the proper lists aren't made from the very beginning and everything can seem rosy, but it can heal your heart too.

Find a comfortable medium. Keep the reminiscing as close to reality as possible. Avoid the pitfall of "remembering" a relationship that does not exist, as it will only lead to further disillusionment and disappointments in the future. This is someone you love, and if you're married, then it's a covenant under God worth This fighting for, but fight with the right weapons. Know your spouse and know your relationship. Don't try to create things that weren't there. Instead, embrace those that were.

When my spouse first deployed I constantly replayed our wedding day in my mind. It wasn't hard; it had only been four months, so the day was still fresh in my mind. And like many couples, I was cognizant of the dreams and hopes that engulf you on the day the represents new beginnings. I replayed all of it—the stresses of the day, the fear, the anxiety, the nervousness, but mostly the peace I had standing beside him and facing him. I recalled the certainty I felt in reciting my marriage vows to a man I knew I wanted to spend my whole life with. I did not disillusion myself. It wasn't the smoothest day in the world, but in the end we came together in joy and peace and felt security without any doubt that we were making the right decision together.

Reminiscing about my wedding day helped me apply those same principles to what I was currently facing in the deployment. It wasn't easy, we weren't thrilled, but in the end we were going to stand together in love and promise to stand by one another through one of life's tribulations. It was our first great test.

To reminisce about your loved one and your time together, especially the good times, is a great tool to getting through this the right way. It keeps your mind focused and your goals through the separation related to your marriage and your future together. It's the easiest way to keep your soldier with you always. No one is going to shut off your mind. Reminiscing brings them back to you in bed at night, at breakfast in the morning, to share your lunch with you mid-afternoon. Duty may have taken your soldier physically, but no one can take him or her from your thoughts and heart.

One of the greatest opportunities you two can share as a couple is reminiscing together. What a beautifully intimate way to get to know one another. I have had the opportunity to really get to know my spouse this way. I can't say it enough—reminisce together. Talk to one another about specific moments, dates, and events. Be raw with each other. Open your heart and share yourself and what was really going on at that time. Utilize this situation; it has not happened by accident. God has allowed this to happen, and it's for a reason. What better time than to make those reasons count under the security of distance and yearning. Both of you are afraid, overwhelmed, and needing to reach out to one another, so ask the questions you were afraid to ask. There's always those moments that you still have questions about, and now is the time to find out. Ultimately this can be one of the deepest experiences the two of you can ever share, and if you make it a habit to reminisce together throughout the deployment, there will be an unbreakable bond that has formed as a result, one that no one will ever be able to take away.

With regard to reminiscing, there's no better advice I can give then to think about your soldier. It keeps him or her with you and real in your life, especially during a time when it may seem easier to forget. I guarantee the rewards are far greater to hold on, and the best way to do that is to keep them alive in your mind. As a soldier I know that no matter how busy a soldier is when deployed to war, he or she is thinking of you.

Regret

This is a very powerful topic for me. Initially I don't believe I fully thought it through as I began writing this portion of the chapter. I considered the act of regret from the emotional perspectives. Regret is something that inevitably will happen to those left behind as they think about their soldiers in terms of the past. However, the Lord has guided me differently as I began to study the truth behind regret.

The truth is simple. The Bible says very little about regret. There must be a reason for that. I can only come to believe that it is not something the Lord condones or encourages. As an initial feeling perhaps it is acceptable, but I believe that if we begin to consider all of our regrets, one of two things are likely to happen.

First, we are going to get so wrapped up in our regrets and what we should not have said and done in the past that we are going to forget about focusing on the future. It is very easy to become one of those people who live their lives stuck in the past. It may not begin with bad intention. On the contrary, it may begin with the best of intentions to make wiser choices in the future, but regret has a magnetic appeal and all of a sudden months have gone by and we find ourselves so stuck on the past that we have done little or nothing to fix our mistakes, improve our circumstances, and change the future.

The second thing we run the risk of doing is completely altering the idea that there is a purpose in our life. God uses our experiences to teach us things and to build us into better people. Life is all about growth and development. Constantly regretting what has happened in the past distorts its purpose in your growth process. Whether it's the growth and development of your marriage or the defining moment in the relationship with your child, the things that have occurred in the past have occurred for a reason, and God doesn't want us to stay stuck on regret. He wants us to keep moving forward and learn from our experiences.

One of the greatest examples of this was the crucifixion of Jesus Christ. What greater time to be engulfed in regret? If ever there were a time to experience regret for a decision, this was it, but instead he asked the Lord to forgive the people, and before he took his last breath the books describe his words of concession. The Son of God himself did not give himself up to regret. Instead he maintained focus on his purpose and trust for his reasons.

Experiencing something as challenging as a deployment makes this vital in maintaining a positive outlook. Don't allow yourself to get sucked into the spiral of regret. Make the lists of concerns and then put your energy and focus into healing and mending what is weak or broken. Keep a sense of purpose, whether it involves fighting for a strong marriage, rebuilding a relationship with your child, or holding on to a best friend. Create the purpose; identify the deficiencies and areas of needed improvement, and work to heal them through ongoing study, communication, and lots of love and prayer.

To reflect, to reminisce, and to regret are fairly inevitable. They will happen at some point, but what you choose to do with those tools are up to you. I can only provide a sense of direction and guidance based on my own experiences and the stories of countless others and how to make these powerful emotions work to heal your relationship and enhance the separation of deployment into a positive experience.

Journal Entry

1. My soldier just left, and the mood between us was …

_____

_____

_____

_____

_____

_____

_____

_____

_____

_____

_____

_____

_____

2. Some of the things that went wrong between us were …

_____

_____

_____

_____

_____

_____

3. Some of things that we handled really well as we prepared for this were ...

_____

_____

_____

_____

_____

_____

_____

_____

4. Our greatest moments to reminisce about as a couple include ...

_____

_____

_____

_____

_____

_____

_____

_____

5. Moments in the past I want to revisit with my soldier include ...

_____

_____

_____

_____

_____

Point to Ponder

Reflection is most important for you as an individual. You must take a moment to look back and identify the reality of your relationship and then make adjustments as needed. Reminiscing is most beneficial for the two of you to do together. It will create a bond and an understanding that may not have been there otherwise. Regret is the behavior to be most cautious with and to give the least amount of time. Don't waste precious energy on regrets. Move forward and work to mend any less than ideal actions or situations from the past. Stay positive and that spirit can't help but leak into all areas of your life.

Chapter 5

Having a Baby Alone

*...and exclaimed to Mary, "You are blessed by
God above all other women, and your child is
blessed." (Luke 1:42).*

*Children are a gift from the Lord; they are a
reward from him. (Ps. 127:3).*

I dedicate this chapter to those expectant
mothers or women who have given birth during
their soldier's deployment. My intention is not to
isolate other readers but to embrace and encourage a
special population of strong women reading this
book. My hopes are also to shed new light on what
this experience is really like for all of those who are
reading this today. We are all different, and what
may be one's suffering could be another's joy, but
that's the beauty of pregnancy. It's not the

divergence of each individual experience, but the unanimous agreement that it is not easy for anyone.

There is a mixed blessing in being pregnant during a deployment. There must be something to it or it wouldn't be occurring so often. Not that I am in any position to make assumptions, but it does seem to be agreed that the majority of pregnant spouses are expecting their babies while their spouse is deployed. Coincidence? I think not.

There are many reasons why this should be viewed as a blessing in disguise. Essentially all babies are a gift from the Lord, and there is something beautiful, a miracle in becoming a parent. It is irrelevant whether this is the first pregnancy or the fifth one. This is a time in your life where the Lord has blessed you with a child. That alone is cause for gratitude and celebration.

As I mentioned at the beginning of the book, I found out I was pregnant around the same time I found out my husband would be deploying. I knew he would leave as I was entering my final trimester, which I considered to be the time I would need him the most. I was initially paralyzed with fear, so much so that I was on the verge of a full-blown anxiety attack. I could not fathom facing a pregnancy and the experience of childbirth alone. It was inconceivable to me, and I was quick to assume I would fail or break down emotionally.

All I could think about was carrying around this big belly and trying to raise my other children, go to work, go to school, manage our day-to-day duties in our home— and I having to do it all alone. I couldn't understand why this was happening to me.

I had a plan. I was supposed to finish my army schooling. I was supposed to get married. I was supposed to arrive at Ft. Bliss, Texas and I was supposed to deploy to Iraq beside my husband. It was all so clear. How many of us out there have reached that point in our lives when we know we have a plan and it's supposed to go off perfectly? Sometimes, my friends, God has another plan for us, and if we're willing to trust in him, he will lead us down the right road. Staring into the innocent green eyes of my infant daughter and kissing my other girls goodnight reminds me of how thankful I am that I did things God's way and not my own way.

Guiltily, I must admit that even after my spouse deployed, I thought very little of how he was feeling about leaving me at the end of my pregnancy. It never really occurred to me that he would be experiencing anything at all. I figured as a man, he couldn't possibly relate to what I was going through which meant he probably thought very little of it, if at all.

How wrong I was. I write this book in hopes that those of you out there reading this, with a baby growing inside of you, don't make the same mistakes I made. His absence through my pregnancy affected us both. It was a great sacrifice we made as a couple for the call of duty to our country. It's an experience that we can never get back, but like anything else, it has its benefits and downfalls. I've listed some things to consider about the absence of Daddy during your pregnancy.

Benefits

1. Pregnant ladies aren't always the nicest, especially at the end of a pregnancy. Many times we suffer through irritation, short tempers, and all-out moodiness. Sometimes we say things we don't mean and hurt those around us. It's an experience that I'm sure most daddies brace themselves through.

2. It's all about me. Pregnancy is a time when we want what we want the way we want it and there's not much room for discussion. So consider this a time when you can eat whatever you want whenever you want, even if he's not exactly keen on the idea of chocolate ice cream for dinner. Oh, and let's not forget, there's no reason to share the TV. Lifetime movie network 24/7! Always a plus.

3. You get all of the pillows and all of the bed to yourself without the guilt of throwing him to the couch … need I say more?

4. Do you really *want* him to see the beyond humanly possible sized ankles? He may be tempted to call the press.

5. Doctors recommend women gain between twenty five and thirty pounds during pregnancy. Some of

us hit that mark midway through the pregnancy. At least if he returns home after the baby's born, we have time to get back to looking how we did before the pregnancy.

Sacrifices

1. There's nothing like Daddy's touch when our back and our feet need a good rub.

2. Sharing baby's kicks inside you and watching your belly grow are moments of such miracle between the two of you.

3. When we go into labor it's very exciting and pretty scary. Who better to comfort you than the one who loves you most?

4. There's nothing like having Daddy paint your toenails, tie your shoes, and help you get out of the car. Some of these things feel nearly impossible when you're on your own.

5. I wish I had a picture of the look on his face every time he noticed my belly growing. It made me feel like the most beautiful woman in the world. I really missed that at the end.

Like anything in life, you take it one day at a time. Focus on the benefits. The only reason I listed the sacrifices is because avoiding the reality doesn't make it go away, and it's important for me to, at the very least, let all of you out there know that you are not alone. Going through a pregnancy alone is not easy. It's not easy at all, but I guarantee that once you get through it, you will be stronger than you ever thought possible.

The Labor Coach

I can't begin to describe the importance of a labor coach. I was very lucky that a fellow soldier, and my very best friend, was willing to step in and be my labor coach. She is one of the most reliable and level-headed people I've ever known. I couldn't have asked for a better coach. Her only request was that I not give birth on the weekend so that at least this way she'd have an excuse to take the day off from work. My contractions began on Saturday night and the baby was born on Super Bowl Sunday; she swore it was a conspiracy.

My labor coach was someone I knew I could count on regardless of time or distance. I made it a point to test that theory by calling her at 3:00 am with regular contractions. She arrived at my house within ten minutes in an army PT (physical training) uniform, at which point I figured we still had some time and recommended we go back to sleep for a few hours more. Pregnant women really are a joy.

She ate breakfast through some of my severest contractions. I'll have to thank the nurse's staff for that one. They recommended we walk around a little bit before I was to be admitted into the labor and delivery ward; she figured it was a good time for breakfast. She told stories, ate her French toast, and giggled a lot. I in turn had visions of ripping out my eyeballs and screaming every known obscenity at her in return. It was a true bonding moment. It's probably a good time to add that she had never given birth. She was a true champion.

We went through the entire experience together. She stood beside me through the catheter, the epidural, the contractions, and the pushing. I will never forget the look on her face when the doctor asked her to hold my leg up in the air as I pushed the baby out. What a friend. She then cut the baby's cord and made sure I was okay.

I can't ever thank her enough for her friendship and support. She is the example of the best kind of girlfriend a girl could ever hope for. There was an unspoken understanding and appreciation between us. I could never have voiced the depth of my gratitude for her decision to be there beside me and support me when I could have ended up all alone. Having her there helped to keep my mind off of my solitude and focus on the miracle of my brand new baby girl.

Choosing a labor coach is a delicate and important decision. Some expectant mothers are very lucky and are able to have family come out and stay with them. For most that's not the case. Hundreds of military spouses are often staying on a post or in a city where they hardly know anyone. This is why it's important to build a support group and make friends. Other military spouses are a great group. Most often they are either going through the same experience or have been through it before and can understand what it's really like. I highly discourage isolating yourself. It's only going to make a difficult situation much worse. We are created to interact and rely on each other, and especially in times of deployment, spouses need to follow suit to the way soldiers live their lives and take care of one another.

Some questions to consider when choosing your labor coach include:

1. Is he or she reliable? Can I count on him or her at any time?

2. Does he or she genuinely care about me and my family?

3. Is this person good under pressure? (Only daddies get permission to pass out in the delivery room.)

4. Will he or she be reachable at any time? Pregnant women are notorious for going into labor in the middle of the night.

Bringing Baby Home

A labor coach's duties don't end once the baby's out. Oftentimes the coach is the one who cuts the baby's cord, helps you get to the bathroom for the first time, and drives the two of you home. I was so lucky to have such a wonderful labor coach that as soon as baby was handed to me, she took pictures with our digital camera and rushed to my home to e-mail them to my husband. She then drove back to the hospital to continue caring for me and the baby. Who could ever ask for a better friend?

The labor coach may even go as far as to spend the first night or two with you just to give you an additional set of hands with the little things around the house. I highly recommend having this even if it's a couple of different friends who pull shifts. It can make all the difference from a comfortable peaceful time where you are able to bond with your baby and master the art of breastfeeding or a stressful, overwhelming time full of tears and anxiety.

For women who have undergone or will undergo a Cesarean section, a buddy through your labor, deliver, and recovery is vital. Most hospitals require someone to be with you at all times you are with the baby, as you are nearly unable to move. Many women forget that a C-section is major surgery, and it's not something you can manage completely on your own with a new baby. It's hard enough trying to get around at all on your own. These are things that must be well thought out and considered as you prepare for the birth of your child.

I won't say that facing a pregnancy and delivery on your own isn't challenging—it is—but it can be done. With the proper planning and awareness of what to expect, it can go very smoothly and create a bond of friendship between two people that would never have occurred otherwise. It's like they say—the Lord works in mysterious ways.

Don't Forget Daddy

Sadly enough, it's pretty easy to forget Daddy during the labor, delivery, and recovery of childbirth, especially when he is so far away, but to do so is very unfair. Many mothers out there will be fortunate enough to never truly know what it's like to be a soldier fighting for freedom in a country where people are trying to kill you every day. They will never experience the suffocation of being stuck within a few-mile radius for more than twelve months of their lives, or how it really feels to completely lose any sense of control in your life. It's a great deal more difficult than most people could ever imagine, and I can't commend our military members enough for their strength, bravery, and sacrifice to do their job for our freedoms.

In return, their loved ones back home have the ability to make a nearly unbearable situation for them just a little bit easier.

Some ways to involve your service member:
- Send them congratulatory cards on being a daddy
- Take a lot of pictures.
- Tape videos of you and the new baby and mail them through the post office or via e-mail.

- Utilize all forms of available technology possible. This includes instant messaging, webcams, e-mail, video teleconferencing—anything you can get your hands on. I guarantee the initiative will be forever appreciated.

- There's nothing like an old-fashioned, handwritten, straight from the heart letter. This is a very hard time for him too, and hearing you express your love and appreciation will make his day the best day in the world.

This isn't an easy time for daddies out there. Many of them feel as though they are letting you down by not being there for you and are somehow already failing as a father by not being there for the birth of their child. They are unable to experience the joy of holding that child for the first time when it's born, or hearing its first cry. This is a very difficult thing for any man to bear, especially when he feels expected to maintain his "military bearing" and remain stoic and unemotional. Now more than ever your baby's father needs your support.

The military has gone to great lengths to implement ways to make it easier for expectant fathers. This includes precedence on the fifteen day rest and recuperation, opportunities to talk to the chaplain, and oftentimes priority on all available telecommunication means. The military is aware of the effects this experience can have on service members and the importance of keeping them involved and informed during such a special occasion. It helps with wartime readiness, morale, and overall effectiveness.

So for all intents and purposes, the military is doing its part, but the emotional duty ultimately falls on those at home.

What You May Be Feeling

It's not unusual to be pretty angry at the world right now. We are all different and will handle this experience in our own way. However, there is strength in numbers, and my hopes are that women out there aren't suffering through guilt as a result of their feelings. Some things may seem taboo, but in reality they are pretty common and you are not alone.

I remember how angry I felt the first week of my daughter's life. I felt cheated and lonely. I had so much love in my heart for this baby and what she represented, but I didn't think it was fair that I had to do it all by myself. There was no one to help me through the late night diaper changes or 2:00 am feedings, and sometimes I just wanted so badly to sleep, but I knew I couldn't.

Please remember that it's okay to be angry. It's okay to feel cheated and overwhelmed. The important thing is not to allow those feelings to control you. There is power in acknowledgement, utilizing whatever form works best. This can include screaming at the top of your lungs from your rooftop, *"I am angry!"* or writing in your journal about your day, or calling up a close, supportive friend and just explaining how you feel. Whichever method works best for you, the first step is acknowledgement. The second is to combat it.

If you are experiencing negative feelings, it's important to assess their severity. I would never make light of the reality of postpartum depression. Some women are affected by it worse than others. Some symptoms of postpartum depression include sadness, lack of energy, trouble concentrating, anxiety, and feelings of guilt and worthlessness. Postpartum depression often affects a woman's well-being and keeps her from functioning well for a longer period of time. Postpartum depression needs to be treated by a physician. Counseling, support groups, and medicines are some things that can help. If you feel that you may be suffering from postpartum depression, it is important to seek medical assistance immediately.

For the rest of us who are simply upset with the unfair roll of the dice, we must remember that we were created by a God of purpose. Nothing happens by accident. There is a greater reason and meaning to this all, and the experience can be that much better once you are able to see it through God's eyes.

Look at your situation and remember the thousands of people in the world who are unable to have children. I don't, in any way, intend to minimize what may be one of the greatest struggles a woman will ever experience. I simply hope to provide a different way to look at this— through the miracle and the beauty of life and all that it represents. It's not easy to go through it alone, but if you are facing giving birth to your baby while the baby's father is deployed, than you have no choice but to be strong, for you and your baby.

Be joyous, for God has given you a special gift, the gift of life, and you now have a little reminder to love, hold, and kiss at night. It is a reminder of one of the bravest people you'll have ever known; your soldier.

Journal Entry

1. I am expecting my baby on (date).

_____

I hope that he/she looks like.

_____

Describe some details. For example, Mommy's
eyes, Daddy's smile, etc.

_____

_____

_____

_____

_____

2. Some things I didn't think I would feel about this
pregnancy are …

_____

_____

_____

_____

_____

_____

_____

_____

_____

_____

3. I must remember to tell "Daddy" about:

_____

_____

_____

_____

_____

_____

_____

_____

_____

_____

Point to Ponder

The Bible talks about how special children are in the eyes of the Lord. He has given us a very special job to love, protect, and care for them. They are a very special gift to us, and we are very lucky to be able to tell them about how brave and honorable their father was when he served in the war.

Chapter 6

Life Deployed: Soldier Issues

*Be strong and courageous, for you will lead my
people to possess all the land I swore to give their
ancestors. Be strong and very courageous…
(Josh. 1:6–7).*

*I command you- Be strong and courageous! Do
not be afraid or discouraged. For the Lord your
God is with you wherever you go (Josh. 1:9).*

I have been very fortunate and very blessed that
I have not experienced a deployment to war in my
short career in the Army. Had my number been
called and had I been required to face that reality,
the two scriptures above would probably have been
one of my greatest sources of comfort. In both the
Old Testament and the New Testament God
continuously promises that he is with you wherever
you go. This is pivotal for me in all areas of life,

and I hope the greatest comfort I can give to anyone reading this is the certainty of knowing that if the soldier you love is deployed tonight, or preparing to deploy, God commanded that we be strong and courageous and trust in the knowledge that we are not alone, for he is with us wherever we go.

In chapter five, I really wanted to focus on a very specific group of people dealing with a deployment: the pregnant wife. In chapter six, I want to do the same, however, this time looking at the other end of the spectrum — the service member. How better for us to cope, trust, and try to understand how best to handle this than to get an idea from their perspective of what it's really like to be deployed.

My research came from a very diverse population of soldiers currently deployed to Iraq. I interviewed males and females of all ranks, married and single.

My goal was to have a truly well-rounded understanding of what it was like for the individual and for the multitude. The results were surprising. Among all the soldiers that responded to my questions, there were many similarities and few differences. I believe this supports the basis of tradition in the military where regardless of color, nationality, gender, or background, or branch, you are trained to come together and operate as one. Everyone ultimately is a hero with one goal, to serve our nation and the people to the left and right of us on the battlefields.

I invite you to learn a little bit as you read this chapter. My suggestions and stories come directly from the soldiers themselves. They were willing to take very precious time to help put together some pertinent information for the masses of family members and loved ones waiting for them, and I dedicate this chapter to those who helped bring it to light. Thank you.

It's Time

I understand the great deal of pride we feel when we put our uniforms on. It's the pride that accompanies the agreement to fulfill our duty to our country. This is an integral part of receiving the news that it's time to pack up and take our place. Regardless of the cause, it's not a service member's luxury to pick and choose which causes they will support and defend and which they will pass on. Instead, they are trained to respect the order of the Commander in Chief, the President of the United States of America, and be ready.

From my perspective as an officer in the Army, and from the responses to my questions for this book, this is not an area where the military suffers. Service members now more than ever have a clear understanding that we are a country at war—a country at war in foreign lands and a country at war for the enduring freedom of innocent people. There is no doubt that receiving the order to deploy comes as no surprise to most everyone in this field. However, upon the arrival of such life-altering news, there are other concerns.

For the single man or woman there's the awkwardness of having to tell their family in hopes that they will understand and support them. Oftentimes parents didn't agree with their son or daughter joining the armed forces in the first place and deployment will only solidify their perspective. This in turn isolates their child when they need them most.

Generally overlooked are the dating relationships. There's usually nothing that can kill a budding romance faster than receiving the news that the prospective romance must be put on hold for a year. This can be very emotionally difficult for them, especially if he or she was carrying high hopes for a future commitment.

For the married service member, family readiness becomes key. The military oftentimes has an identified group put in place at the unit level. These groups consist of all of the spouses of those in the unit. The intent of the organization is to provide support during times of field training, which can last several weeks, or wartime deployments. However, it's not a secret that many spouses are reluctant to join these organizations filled with what they consider to be strangers, and instead they become solely reliant on their loved one. This in turn places additional responsibilities on a the military member to ensure that not only must they be physically, emotionally, and mentally ready for the upcoming deployment, but so must their spouse. Issues like money, childcare, and where the spouse will live become a concern. And now they are trying to figure it all out on their own as a matter of pride.

If you are married to a service member, one of the greatest things you can do for him or her is create a plan regarding the circumstances if he or she is to deploy. Include monthly expenses, daily schedules, living arrangements, childcare providers, etc. If a service member knows their loved ones will be prepared and able to care for things in their absence it will alleviate a great deal of stress and pressure and allow them to shift their focus to their own readiness for one of the greatest challenges they will ever face.

Life at War

A day doesn't pass in the news world where there isn't some mention of Iraq or Afghanistan, the war, or the different events occurring over there. It's constant, it's daily, and in today's society it's become somewhat monotonous. I believe that the realities of the war and the daily challenges and sufferings have stopped affecting many of us in the United States because it's become a part of our everyday lives. Sadly, the war on freedom and its effects has become something as predictable as the weather on the daily news.

I wanted to offer a newer perspective. It was important to me to get feedback from the people at the forefront while they were still deployed. This would alleviate any opportunity to block out the reality around them or allow their mind to soften to how it truly felt while they were there. All accounts that I offer in this book were given to me during real-time war operations. They responded to my questions while they were deployed and living these experiences from day to day. Across the board, regardless of rank, gender, or job, some general comments made by all included the following.

1. The importance of mail
2. How quickly time passes if you choose to stay busy
3. The "Groundhog Day" effect
4. The general fear upon first arrival
5. The hardest part of the deployment is losing one of your own.
6. Make the most of your time with fitness, financial, or educational goals.

The importance of mail

This one is very near and dear to my heart. I have had the ability to see it from both sides. I remember being at basic training in South Carolina. The first night of mail call my name wasn't called. I had to go straight to bed so that no one would see me cry. I was devastated and felt disappointed and let down by those I believed loved me most.

I've also been the spouse left behind. Having to manage twelve-hour workdays, nightly college classes, daily housework duties that get piled up for the weekend, and now sending a package or a letter seems like a greater task than one could ever have imagined. Considering the purchasing of contents, packing the box, waiting in line, filling out all the required forms, it may seem ridiculously simple until you have to do it yourself.

Ultimately this is reality point blank. Our loved ones need mail. It can be a card, a letter, or a box filled with junk food that they will in turn hand out to others that look on enviously. The contents are one thing; the gesture is another. Yet I can assure you the gesture goes a much longer way than the contents.

In an environment surrounded by acquaintances and friends, bosses and subordinates, deployed military and civilians need something from the ones that love them. The simplest letter offers hope, regeneration, and optimism. It's a reminder that there is a life outside this war and a home to return to. It reminds the loneliest person that they are not alone, and there is someone taking the time to reach out to them. And most importantly, when they are surrounded by their peers and their care packages, they become included. I can't say it enough—it isn't easy, but find the time. Write to your deployed service member and send packages. Such a small token of appreciation goes a long way.

How quickly time passes if you choose to stay busy

One thing you can trust when you serve in the military, especially deployed in war, time will fly. Military leaders are trained to keep their subordinates very busy. This will alleviate much undue anxiety. Time is not their friend, especially now as deployments are being extended from twelve to fifteen months. This isn't easy for anyone. Those deployed, especially the younger ones, are at major risk for developing emotional disorders. They face more stress related to a lack of decision making and control than senior leaders. Keeping them very busy is essential in making the most of their time out there. It helps to ensure that time flies by and gives them a sense of purpose and greatness.

Truthfully, many deployed to war today find their sense of purpose, patriotism, and existence doing their part in a wartime mission. If they remain occupied and filled with work, they will validate their piece in the bigger picture and the months will fly by. It's not uncommon for those deployed to have very little concept of the day of the week or current time. The average service member works six to seven days a week, eight- to twelve-hour shifts. That alone is a tremendous tribute to their unending dedication and commendable sense of duty to the mission.

The "Groundhog Day" effect

I'm not really sure at this point how many loved ones and family members can really understand the level of what soldiers lovingly refer to as the "groundhog day" effect. This stems from the movie starring Bill Murray where every day is the same thing once again. This is very much the case in wartime missions, especially those associated with noncombat arms responsibilities.

Oftentimes people don't realize the numbers of service members it takes to fulfill duties in food service, communications, maintenance, and intelligence—just as many as it does to kick in doors and clear rooms. The "groundhog day" effect is especially true for those combat support and combat service support jobs the military offers. Their mission in Iraq consists of daily routines that do not change. These people spend each day doing the same functions, compiling the same reports, analyzing the same data, eating chow at the same time, with very little room for change. These particular living conditions have effects all on their own. All things considered, there is another population of people who experience this same lifestyle of monotony. We call them prisoners, and we house them in our correctional facilities.

Some fears on their part can consist of the break in routine. It is essential once they turn home that family come to understand the reality of this and keep them occupied, even if they're sorting socks. Idle time can be trained service member's greatest enemy. Remember that they have spent the greatest span of their last year doing the same thing day after day, and altering that routine brings challenges all on its own.

The general fear upon first arrival

Hundreds of thousands of Americans are very fortunate that they will never have to experience what it's like to stand around on foreign soil and wait for a bus to pick you up and take you to the American camp (a.k.a. the forward operating base [FOB]) in deeply hostile territory. For most upon arrival in Kuwait (the first stop for those heading to Iraq), especially first time arrivals, soldiers are terrified. They avoid sleep, peer out windows, fear showers, all a result of readiness of a potential impending attack. Regardless of whether you know you will most likely as part of today's military, the "knowing" and the "being there" are two totally different things.

From the get go upon arrival they are required to face the reality of being a part of a global war. This could mean the ultimate sacrifice of their lives, or the sacrifice of a year of their life. Either way, special considerations must be in place for providing   extra   love   and   security   upon redeployment. Can you imagine having to reintegrate into daily life after spending a large portion of your day listening to gunfire in the distance and feeling the buildings shake around you when the enemy engages in mortar attacks or a vehicle-borne IED goes off? These are powerful experiences and memories that take time to heal from. Provide your loved one with a great deal of patience, love, and understanding. Most often the greatest gift you can give is just a willingness to listen.

Make the most of your time with fitness, financial, or educational goals

The goal-oriented strategy was popular among those deployed. I asked all of the soldiers I interviewed what their advice would be to fellow comrades preparing to deploy for the very first time. All of them agreed that being goal-oriented was the key to mental and emotional stability. I believe this applies to those who are deployed as well as to those family members back home.

The war in Iraq and Afghanistan is very different from the wars we have fought throughout the nation's history. Our soldiers are smack in the middle of heavily populated cities and conducting patrols on streets full of buildings and traffic. In the military we've termed this new type of environment urban warfare. The way we train, the uniforms we wear, strategies and emplacement are all different and are continually shifting to gain the advantage in the environment to which those deployed operate.

Nowadays, the military has implemented various morale, welfare, and recreational activities to assist in alleviating some of the stresses of everyday life while deployed. U.S. FOBs have everything from shopping areas, gyms, and basketball courts, to computer labs, fast food vendors, and recreational facilities. The soldiers I spoke with are now in the transition phase preparing to redeploy. Their unit was extended beyond the twelve month mark, and the universal advice given to others preparing to arrive in country was to stay busy.

Specifically, they mentioned the importance of utilizing the facilities offered. Go to the gym as often as possible. Build your strength and renew your mind through online classes or available online research. Take a difficult situation and make the most of it by applying some personal incentives as well as the contribution to the aid of the people we are defending. The military offers financial compensation for deployed soldiers. Use that extra money to secure your family's future or your own. Invest wisely, and take advantage of the opportunity to focus solely on the betterment of your situation and your family's situation. Ultimately, take the challenge you currently face and maximize this time for the good in your life. That makes it all worth it, both for you and your loved one.

The hardest part of a deployment is losing one of your own

Across the board, when asked, those currently deployed expressed to me that the most difficult thing they had experienced was the loss of a fellow service member. This was hands down the most unified and agreed upon response. This was not only the tragedy that impacted them the most, but in turn, repetition never made it easier.

When you make the transition from civilian to military you undergo many changes. Things you never believed you could do before become easy and natural. Whether it's drinking water directly from a bathroom sink or ruck marching over seven miles with thirty pounds on your back, infantry-type activities are so unremitting that they become second nature. The exception to this is the acceptance of losing a fellow brother/sister in arms.

When a unit is deployed to war, they take on the existence of a second family, a large family that is then broken down into battalions, companies, and platoons. Combat support companies are then divided into specialized sections. So, for example, all of the food service personnel belong to a section, the personnel management is divided into a section, the area in charge of supply is a section, etc. What happens then is these soldiers are living and working with the same people, oftentimes in a close-quartered environment day in and day out for an entire year. Most of us couldn't fathom spending that much time with our own spouse, much less a coworker. This, however, is their reality. Whether it's ideal or not, they have no choice. This in turn creates that "brotherly" (females included) bond that is so apparent between these great heroes, especially once they've redeployed back home. There is a great bond because of all the time and experience they've shared.

When the reality of war is faced and soldiers are forced to deal with the death of one of their own, it is very sobering. Someone that they may have interacted with on a daily basis is now gone, never to return. It could be someone greatly admired, very dedicated, a leader to many. Or it may have been a valorous, young, and innocent hero; regardless, the impact is felt throughout. The reality is that someone back home will have to face one of the greatest losses they will ever face again. Families will now be missing one of their own. It is a deep realization felt by all that are working in the war zone today.

Advice for the Loved Ones

Patience, patience, and more patience. This is the key to helping your loved one. You may never fully understand what it was like for him or her or what he or she has been through, but they need you now more than ever. They need you to reach out as much as possible from the beginning to the end.

Later in the book I will cover some tips and strategies in preparation for their return home, but I hope to have conveyed some important underlying messages as you read what they themselves had to say.

Ultimately they need to connect with the ones they love back home, whether it's through letters and mail or the Internet. Their schedule at war is very demanding, exhausting, and emotionally draining at times. Be mindful that it isn't always easy for them to pick up a phone and call their loved ones. In some cases they skip out on meals to instead spend the time calling home. This is just one example of their need for connection.

In knowing that, ensure that phone calls and letters are as pleasant as possible. There is no greater gift to give someone you love at war than encouragement and the power of good news.

Journal Entry

1. After reading this chapter, I spoke to my loved one. He or she could mostly relate to …

_____

_____

_____

_____

_____

_____

2. Some of my plans while they're deployed include:

Childcare_____

I will live_____

Our monthly bills total: _____

3. Some goals I hope to accomplish in their absence include:

_____

_____

_____

_____

_____

_____

Point to Ponder

You are very fortunate. However, you are linked to your service member. Whether it's your cousin, son, daughter, or spouse is irrelevant. You have been blessed with the opportunity to see greatness at its best. The average person could not fathom the thought of sacrificing a day of their lives the way that our best trained military members do. Show them you love them by offering the ultimate in appreciation and compassion. Plaques, letters, videos, and care packages are just some examples of saying thank you. These are regular people who have stepped up to a greater call and have earned our unending admiration and support.

Chapter 7

Rest and Relaxation: My Saving Grace

*I don't mean to say that I have already achieved
these things or that I have already reached
perfection! But I keep working toward that day
when I will finally be all that Christ Jesus saved me
for and wants me to be (Phil. 3:12).*

*I am leaving you with a gift - peace of mind and
heart. And the peace I give isn't like the peace the
world gives. So don't be troubled or afraid.
(John 14:27).*

What Is "R&R" for the Military?

In today's military R&R (an acronym
representing rest and recuperation) is a very often-
used and well understood term. It's a term that
describes the fifteen days of leave given to a service

75

member to go anywhere in the world while he or she is deployed to support the war on terror. Many of them often forget that this is a privilege, not a right and the leave time must be granted by their chain of command based on mission requirements, but generally military leaders do all they can to afford as many as possible an opportunity to utilize this program.

It has been proven that allowing them an opportunity to return to their families and temporarily reintegrate with them deeply improves both military and family morale. This very special time provides both the service member and their families an opportunity to reconnect and be together. It also gives everyone something to generally look forward to besides the redeployment home after twelve to fifteen months away.

R&R can be assigned at any time during the deployment. Some are given slots as early as sixty days after deploying. Others don't take their leave time until they've been deployed ten months. So the myth that you are guaranteed to go on leave during the middle of the deployment is generally not the case.

Because of this, they and their loved ones are faced with many challenges. Having to handle the realities of a "visit" home can place a great deal of stress on families and the timing of that visit even more so.

Facing "R&R" at the Beginning of a Year Away

This may seem like worst-case scenario, but with anything else in life, it really doesn't have to be. Going on leave early on can be whatever you make of it. There is always a bright side if you're just willing to see it.

Some service members actually choose to go on R&R early. This includes those who are expecting babies early on and are coming home to see be present for the birth, family special events, or best-case scheduling with a spouse. For more and more dual military couples, they may be deployed to different locations in Iraq or Afghanistan or Kuwait, and in order to time their leave together, one is required to take it early. For others it may just be a simple case of luck. A slot was available early on and their name was randomly chosen to fill that slot. It happens. However it may have come about, this is your circumstance, and you must best prepare for it as necessary.

On the bright side:

• Your loved one still may be adjusting to life at war and hasn't yet changed too much from the person you remember.

• For planned returns you can focus on the reason he or she is back so early and celebrate.

• For the service member, he or she can enjoy his or her time, make the most of it, and then redeploy back to war, focusing solely on the mission at hand. His or her leave is up until it's time to come back home.

- They are back for a short time—who cares when it happens! They're back!

On the down side:

- Offer your loved one a lot of support and encouragement if they begin to feel there's nothing left to look forward to.

- Just as you're beginning to acclimate yourself and adjust to being away, you come back to remember all the things you're missing at home.

- It may seem like a very long year ahead once there's no more leave to enjoy.

Facing "R&R" Near the End of the Deployment

Taking leave toward the end of a deployment is a fifty-fifty deal. Some much prefer it this way. Others truly dread the idea of having to wait. For those who are dreading it, they were either one of those "luck of the draw" names or they too have some timed event they're expecting that they based their leave on, wanting to attend. And for the other half, they are truly looking forward to just waiting and then going on leave, returning back, and shortly thereafter returning home.

On the bright side:

- You've almost finished your commitment and toward the end you can begin focusing on the benefits of hard work.

• The last part of the deployment will go really quickly, as you'll be traveling most of the time.

• As I mentioned before, they're back for a short time. Who cares when it happens! They're back!

On the down side:

• It's easy to develop a loss of hope when it seems that your break time is so far down the road.

• It's possible to reach a mental burnout point before you're able to get home and be with your loved ones.

No matter what, above all else, try to keep in mind that when it happens should not be the focus. This is a celebrated event. Thank God above for allowing your soldier to come back, and show him or her a lot of patience and understanding as he or she enjoys a short time with the ones he or she loves.

Preparing for R&R

My husband came home after eight months of being away. We were very fortunate in that he was able to come back the month I had most hoped for. It was five months after I had given birth to our baby girl. This was time I had wanted to get back into shape and when I believed our daughter would still be infant-like but responsive to her father as opposed to asleep all the time. However, as much as it was a true blessing to have him home with us, it was a great challenge for me. I knew that I didn't get to keep him; I'd have to give him back to the cause after fifteen days. I couldn't think of anything in the world that was harder than that.

For many loved ones out there this is really very difficult. You want to celebrate your soldier. You want to hug them and kiss him or her and enjoy every minute he or she is home, but it's not uncommon to have a shadow looming over you during this time, a shadow that represents the second loss patiently awaiting its opportunity to rear its ugly head and reminding you that he or she isn't home for good. He or she must leave again. This can be extremely difficult.

For so many it may seem as though their loved one tested the fates the first time and came out okay, but who's to say they'll be so lucky the second time around? For others the bond may be so strong between the soldiers and their loved ones that they begin reconnecting and reintegrating immediately and then over two weeks later when it's time to go back, that loved one is functioning as an everyday member of the family again with daily duties and responsibilities. In this case the family is forced to relearn how to be independent again, and this can be very difficult, especially for young children.

I can't stop reiterating the celebratory aspect of this time. The military's offering of R&R is a gift and a great opportunity to enjoy a very special time with the ones you love. Make the most of it, and enjoy it for all it's worth.

There are important things to consider in preparing for R&R that may help to make the most of this time for a soldier and his or her family.

Don't plan too much

It's easy to become inspired. So much time apart can give one a lot of time to create daily itineraries of things to do while they're back. All of a sudden you're faced with the "well, I've always wanted to see" ... and the "I've never traveled to" ... and before you know it you have a fifteen day itinerary full of things to do.

While it's a great idea in nature, there's a slight problem with filling all of military members' days with fun-filled events full of action-packed experiences. I revert back to the old adage—time flies when you're having fun. And while, yes, fun is the desired end state, too much of it may make such precious time go so quickly that it's time to leave when it seems like they just got there. So my advice is relax, enjoy time's greatest reward—merely being together. Whether it's your son, daughter, husband, or wife, this is time to just enjoy his or her company and let him or her unwind. Allow the days to roll slowly by; it will be appreciated all the more.

Think about all they're giving up

This is a common pitfall and one I fell into myself. Unless you have deployed to war past or present, it is very difficult to really understand what life is like. Even in this modern-day battlefield where the military have set up mini "towns" called FOBs on known hostile areas with many modern facilities, it is still war. They are still far, far away from everyone they love and living in a country where they are the minority under some very difficult conditions.

As you plan your time, take his or her interests and desires into consideration. I can virtually guarantee that for so many of them who are working every single day at a unusually fast pace, all they are looking forward to is some relaxed quiet time with very few demands. They have a clearer ability to understand that this is very short, limited time to themselves and their greatest need is to simply decompress from the endless physical and mental demands on them at work.

If they like sports, let them watch sports on TV or go outside and play sports. If your wife is coming home from Iraq and her favorite thing to do is dress up and go dancing, then take her dancing.

As much as this is a sacrifice for all involved, and the families and the loved ones suffer as well, these fifteen days are like a life blood to many military members, and even if they may not say it, I guarantee they have some ideas about how they want to spend their time, and it is important to get them to talk about it.

Reduce the visitors as much as possible

I can just begin to see the hundreds of people that just read that top sentence and shook their head in disbelief. "What do you mean?" you may be asking yourself. My "person" has so many people that love him or her and want to see them. What an opportune time. Besides, how can they not appreciate all the attention? I know, I know, I understand the logic. And let me reiterate that everyone is different, and so ultimately it's most important to talk to your loved one about this as soon as he or she is back in the United States and see how they feel about it. But generally I may just be stating what many of those deployed are afraid to say themselves out of fear they'll hurt someone's feelings.

While deployed the thought of a lot of people around them and visiting family and having family come over and stay may sound like a terrific idea, especially while they're deployed and are not around any family and are feeling fairly isolated. However, actually coming home may be a completely different story. What may seem as genuine interest and curiosity about the war to a family member may make the one actually deployed feel as though they are under a lot of pressure. There is the sense of expectation and performance. Knowing that family may be expecting certain behaviors or answers to questions is difficult to face because they are then never allotted a time to fully relax during a time scheduled for exactly that.

There is also a general desire to want to please everyone else and be non argumentative toward family plans, but the result is being pulled in many different directions by well meaning loved ones. This in turn creates an environment of stress and resentment, however unintentional. It's bad business for the ones we love. So again, while it's different for everyone, take my cue and ask your loved one once he or she is back in the United States if they feel ready to tackle all of the visitors or if all the visitation can be scheduled at the end of the deployment, when they return home instead.

KISS

This is another famous military acronym. It means keep it simple ... sweetie. In other words, be ready to receive your loved one and follow their lead. I can guarantee the first couple of days will be difficult as they adjust back to the time difference. This will most likely include a whole lot of sleeping. Let them rest; they need it. Most people I spoke to in researching for this book all had the common desire to just relax during R&R. Their greatest pleasure was just watching the ones they love around them and merely absorbing the reality that they're back home, even if just for a short time.

For others it's difficult to watch how life has continued while they've been away. Being deployed to war and doing the same type of work day in and day out can seem like you're stuck in time too. Coming back and seeing life move forward around you isn't easy for many. That's normally when the realization hits them regarding how much "life" they really are missing. Be patient with if this happens, and try to include them in day to day duties so that they know they're still included as part of the life they knew before they went off to war.

What about Me?

Believe me; I understand that in times like these we often get sidetracked thinking of the one deployed and so easily we forget ourselves. Or as well-meaning friends

Helping someone else prepare for their loved one's visit from afar, we easily set focus on their needs and wants and forget about the families and all their sacrifice and struggles. This is a delicate time for you too.

Think about this. For the last one, three, eight, or ten months, however long it may have been, you have been forced to accept the reality that someone you love is living thousands of miles away in harm's way and there's nothing you can do about it. But there is something. In fact, there is a lot you can do to ease this time and come out of it stronger, wiser, and better able to appreciate the freedoms and the luxury we enjoy every day. Well, I'm not wealthy, you say to yourself. No, perhaps not, but considering the probable conditions your loved one is living in, having your own private bathroom can be a luxury in itself.

Make the time you are apart count. If this is the first time your son or daughter has ever left home, use this time to truly put your faith and trust in God to protect him or her. For everyone who's reading this today, I urge you, don't use valuable mental energy worrying about your loved one not returning home. Instead, focus on the positive. In the book of Job, Job claims that which I have feared the most has come upon me. Don't let this happen to you; don't allow your greatest fears to come upon you. Envision your loved one stepping off the plane and returning home to be with everyone that loves them.

Tips to consider as the receiving party (that means you)

• *Don't overwhelm yourself!* Relax, relax, relax! I can't express enough the most important thing for them is just being in your close proximity. They won't really notice much else unless, of course, it's pointed out.

• *Don't plan anything that is going to leave you stressed while they're at home.* No one wants to feel like a burden to their family and friends. If they feel that their presence is causing you stress and discomfort, they are going to distance themselves.

Some people do this by returning to their local post and being with other military members. This is really a worst case scenario.

• *Prepare for the visit two to three weeks out.* This allows enough time to get laundry done, food purchased, the car washed prior to their arrival. This way all you have to do is enjoy them once they arrive home.

• *Let yourself feel.* If you're tired, angry, or frustrated it's okay. This isn't easy on anyone. Talk about it. Voice your frustrations and your concerns. I never recommend shouting matches. If you really feel the need to scream and yell, put a pillow beside them and pretend he or she is the pillow. I must warn you, this may be followed by the serious bellyaches from laughing, but at least you're able to get it all off your chest without hurting anyone's heart and the two of you can talk it over afterward.

• *Plan at least one truly special bonding night.* This is good for everyone involved. If it's a spouse that's away, this should be a night of heart to heart talks, good reminiscing, and some future planning. If this is your family member, then what better opportunity to have some family bonding? Reminisce about memories of their childhood. Remind them how proud you are. Talk about all the qualities that they possess that has taken them to such a great position of leadership and self-sacrifice. Not everyone can make it, but they did!

• *Take the time to cherish time for what it is—constantly moving.* We can't stop time, so just enjoy every minute you're given. Don't let your loved one return back to war without telling them everything you really wanted to say. There are no better words to say then I love you and I'm proud of you. It's universal.

There are no golden rules. Unfortunately, I can't wave my magic wand and make this the most glorious time for all involved. I wish I could, but ultimately the responsibility falls on those facing it and living it every day. I did. Facing a deployment was my life, and living through it day in and day out has been one of the greatest challenges I've ever encountered, and through my experiences and the shared experiences of others deployed, I am able to offer some understanding and advice. My only hope is that by putting what I say to use in your situation this very special time of R&R is utilized to its fullest and brings both you and your loved one closer than ever.

Journal Entry

1. My _____is coming home on _____
for R & R.

2. As I think about them walking through the door I
feel and I really want to say

_____

_____

_____

_____

_____

_____

_____

_____

_____

_____

3. I spoke to my service member today and they
mentioned that during R&R they would like to …

_____

_____

_____

_____

_____

_____

_____

_____

_____

Point to Ponder

How fortunate we are in today's modern battlefield that we are able to enjoy this designated rest and recuperation time with our loved ones. This was not the case in our country's previous wars. There was no e-mail, no instant messaging, no given R&R time. People were forced to live on grace and hope alone. All politics aside, this is about those we care about. This is about those who have answered the call of duty and about us as those left behind to love and support them. Enjoy the time you're given together. Make every moment count. And rest assured that you have given love to the fullest no matter what happens in the future. Now is what counts. Make it yours!

Chapter 8

The Last 90 Days

I think you ought to know, dear friends (brothers), about the trouble we went through in the province of Asia. We were crushed and completely overwhelmed, and we thought we would never live through it. In fact, we expected to die. But as a result, we learned not to rely on ourselves, but on God who can raise the dead. And he did deliver us from mortal danger. And we are confident that he will continue to deliver us. He will rescue us because you are helping by praying for us. As a result, many, will give thanks to God because so many people's prayers for our safety have been answered (2 Cor. 1:8–11).

First of all I must say to you, *congratulations!* This is it! The last stretch. I know it feels like this time would never come, but it is finally here—the final three months before you are once again reunited with your loved one. All of the sacrifice, the loneliness, the endless hours of worry and concern for your loved one's well being in a war zone is almost over. However, I must warn everyone who reads this that while this is a time of joy and preparation for the big event, these last three months may also seem like the most challenging portion of the deployment.

Emotions are running high, anxiousness is taking over, and reality is setting in. So while I encourage everyone to remain excited, positive, and look forward to the end of this experience, I can only be honest in admitting that it will not be easy. These next three months will require a newfound patience and understanding, a game plan, and a great deal of prayer.

I would like to share a few possible challenges that a waiting loved one may face during this wonderful and difficult time. As I've mentioned before and will continue to reinforce, everyone is different. Every person deployed in today's armed forces is bringing with him or her a completely different set of values, life experiences, and ways of coping. What may apply to one family may have absolutely nothing to do with another. Therefore, I encourage all my readers to review the different scenarios and apply the theories and strategies to their own particular situation. Individualize your plan for your unique person, based on what you two are going through together, and ultimately you can never go wrong when you ask for guidance from above. I've chosen to segment that last ninety days of a deployment because I was able to experience for myself, as well as witness from friends whose loved ones were deployed, the impact the last three months has not only on the service member but on friends and family as well. This is a significant time, and it posed different challenges than any other time during the separation.

The last three months were probably the most emotionally impacted months for my husband and I. Tensions were high as we debated back and forth on when he would return, and I was really beginning to get very anxious as I could feel every day pass. There were times it appeared to be going slower and slower. However, I also remember this time as the point where my husband and I reached a newfound closeness. During the last three months we had come realize a lot of our difference and perspectives, we had reached agreements and compromises on most of our daily issues, and we had accepted the reality of the deployment and the fact that it was almost over. And so we utilized a lot of the final three months as sort of a "wrapping up" period, where we were able to maximize the last stretch of talk time and began to really solidify our relationship, accept the changes that were bound to happen as a result of our separation, and begin preparing for some of the things we would be facing once he came home.

It was definitely a distinguished period of time in the deployment and one that deserves to be properly segmented. And so I offer some foresight on things that may be yet to come as you begin to enter the final stretch, as well as some help and advice for those who are currently in it and living it every day.

Emotions Are High

During the last ninety days, a flood of emotions can begin to invade all correspondence between the one deployed and his or her family. There are so many different expectations, hopes, and dreams. Hundreds of lonely nights have passed. Some have been filled with loss and sorrow, others with rage and vengeance. All of them share one thing in common; the desire to go home. No matter how brave, how proud, or how determined to win, I can guarantee that just about everyone deployed to battle goes to bed at night wishing they were home. It is human nature and a testament to the true strength and determination that the military members are able to make it every day, despite their feelings, with a renewed sense of motivation and purpose. This is what makes them heroes.

During the final three months of the deployment service members begin to develop anxiousness. For some going home is all they can think about. They're staring at their countdown calendars every hour and imagining all the things they are going to do when they get home. Going home is all they can talk about. They drive their fellow "battle buddies" crazy with continued discussions on the road trips, the vacations, the parties, and all the great things they're going to do once they get there. Getting home becomes nearly an obsession, and every day seems to drag longer and longer. These are the ones who begin packing two months in advance and have probably unpacked and repacked at least five times before they actually get on the plane.

These are the ones who feel they have a great life back home. They are normally involved in a committed relationship, or married, and may or may not have children. These can also be the ones who feel they have left things unsettled at home when they left. This can be troubled relationships or financial issues, or a college education. Regardless, it is something pressing in their lives that they feel they must get back home to. For reservists and the national guard, this type of behavior can be very common as these are men and women who are more accustomed to a normal civilian lifestyle than a vastly different military lifestyle and become very anxious to get back to their normal lives at home.

Military members dealing with a great deal of anxiousness are at risk of emotional breakdowns where there are changes, which are virtually guaranteed, to their schedule for redeployment. Their loved ones must remain extremely patient when their highs are high and their lows are low.

Their heart is in the right place, but the anxiousness and anticipation of getting back can be overwhelming, causing them to be a bit radical these last three months. These same people are susceptible to emotional difficulties during extensions and last minute changes. More than ever they need peace and strength from their loved ones.

It is important for their family members to remain calm and stable. There needs to be an emotional balance when dealing with a highly anxious service member. Families and friends have to strive toward off-setting the high energy with tranquility. This will help keep them from overreacting during moments of contention or frustration. It will also help to keep things in perspective. Time cannot be stopped, and loved ones will be waiting patiently until they come home.

When No One at Home Is Waiting

I remember watching an episode of *Army Wives* one lonely Sunday evening. This show tended to be one of the cruelest measures of punishment I could give myself while my husband was deployed, but to be honest, I couldn't help it. I tried to watch it every single week. I remember this one particular episode that really touched my heart. In it there were these two soldiers stepping off the plane as they had just arrived home from a tour in Iraq. Their fellow soldiers were beginning to leave in the arms and embraces of family members. Balloons had been released and were floating into the sky, and confetti was scattered over the floor as evidence of the celebrations that had taken place only moments before. Families were walking away with smiles on their faces, so enamored with their loved ones' return that no one seemed to notice the two that had been left alone. Apparently with no one there to receive them or welcome them home, they realized all they had at that moment was each other, and they nodded at one another in mutual understanding as they picked up their bags and began to walk away. Fortunately, in the show the post commander noticed the situation, and he and his wife approached them, shook their hands, wishing them a job well done, and escorted them away. In the show it turned out to be a fairly happy ending. In real life, it never really is.

The reality is a bit more like a sergeant whose sister I once worked with. I remember her coming to work one day pretty upset. She had seemed distracted all morning, and finally I was able to ask her about it. She shared with me her frustration about not having been able to take some time and travel to Fort Hood, Texas, where her brother had just arrived from Iraq. I could understand this, except her missing his arrival wasn't the entire cause of her dismay. In actuality she was upset because his live in girlfriend who was pregnant with his child had been unable to make it, as well leaving her younger brother to return from his third tour to Iraq all alone at the receiving station. There was no one there to tell him congratulations or that they were happy he had made it home, safe and out of harm's way. On the contrary, after spending thirty minutes looking for his fiancé, he finally gave up and called a taxi cab to take him home. My friend was really hurting as she thought about her younger brother and what he went through as he watched everyone get picked up by their loved ones, and he was faced with the reality that at that very moment, he could never have felt more alone in his life.

My suggestion is simple. Regardless of the situation, despite what may have occurred in the past, if there is anything that can be done to avoid someone having to return home with no one there to receive him or her, do it. Make the sacrifice; I promise it will be worth it. I understand that there are times in intimate relationships when you and your loved one have decided to go separate ways, or they're your child and you haven't spoken to them since he or she deployed, or perhaps mistakes have been made and the wounds are still open, but this is a time to be as selfless as life will allow. Go above and beyond to ensure that you or someone who cares about him or her is there to welcome them home. I can't begin to describe the loneliness and disappointment of returning to the country you were willing to give your life to defend, and there's no one there to care about you and welcome you home.

If there is any way to avoid this, do so, and show America's brave men and women that they are not alone in their fight for freedom and their sacrifice is appreciated.

The System Isn't Perfect

The return home isn't easy. The military is not perfect. It is comprised of people just like you and me, and sometimes we make mistakes, and sometimes decisions need to be changed. The return home is a major challenge for the military's leaders. There are hours of logistical planning that go into the coordination of returning millions of dollars worth of equipment and thousands of people back to the United States. It isn't an easy task, and I feel sympathetic for the leaders who are tasked to make these decisions. One thing that can be virtually guaranteed is change, and these changes can drive a person crazy.

Ideally military leaders want to allow the unit to return to the United States as soon as possible, but there are many factors that go into these proceedings. Some of these things include the arrival of a new unit to take the place of the current one and of course the training and transitioning time required for the new units. There is the coordination of flight schedules, cleaning and maintenance of the equipment, and property accountability. It is essential for the U.S. military to safeguard its weapons and defense assets in order to protect itself from the enemy, and so a great deal of time is dedicated to ensuring that all of the weapons, equipment, and sensitive items are verified individually before a unit can redeploy.

These are all factors that can become transparent during those last three months of a deployment. All people want to do is get home, and their frustrations can be compounded when they are receiving a lot of pressure from home to get there. It isn't easy for our military to set their minds on a specific date of return and to later be told two days beforehand that they will have to stay another week. This can be traumatic, and most have learned early on to adapt to change and remain flexible when it comes to matters of travel. It's the best way to survive and not have a mental breakdown.

On April 11, 2007, Defense Secretary Robert Gates announced that there would be an extension for units serving in Iraq from twelve to fifteen months. This affected over one hundred thousand soldiers and created the longest combat tours since World War II. This affected my soldier. I was devastated when I received the news that my husband's unit was going to have to stay in Iraq two months longer than originally planned. I clearly remember our conversation the day I found out. Our youngest daughter was three months old, and I told my husband that as soon as she turned four months old and I was once again deployable I was going to request an opportunity to deploy to Iraq and serve with his unit. Needless to say, he was not pleased. After some debate, we both agreed that it was not in our family's best interest that I willingly leave our children and join the war in Iraq; I would have to deal with the news as best I could and continue to do my part and provide my husband the strength and support he needed from me.

This extension affected many units already deployed in Iraq and many families that were preparing for their loved one's arrival on a specific date. I can only begin to imagine the tears that were shed and the fists that were pounded into the wall as service members were forced to be mentally tough and accept their current fates. This extension was an example of a major change to a redeployment schedule, and although it may not be this significant, a difference in the future, changes to a redeployment schedule can and should be expected.

I urge my readers to please be patient and understanding. As difficult as this is for you, it is even harder for those anxious to get home. During those last two or three weeks the waiting becomes endless; time couldn't possibly move slower. All they can do during this very difficult time is wait and attempt to stay busy by watching movies, playing sports, working out, and using the computer centers if they're available. Don't be surprised if your loved one sounds bored, anxious, frustrated, or disinterested in things. He or she is merely doing their best to cope with a difficult situation and the reality that very little of their life is in their control. This is the time to offer gentleness, words of encouragement, and a positive voice through a stressful period.

I Don't Feel the Same

This isn't nearly as rare as we may think. So many romantically involved couples that are separated as a result of a deployment go through moments toward the end of a deployment when they begin to question whether they still feel the same about the person they last saw many months ago. Regardless of whether it's a husband or boyfriend who is the one left behind or a wife or girlfriend, anyone can reach a point after such a long period of time apart where they begin to question if too much time has gone by and things have changed.

This is natural—absolutely natural. Chances are it has been a long time and things have changed. Many spouses find a new sense of independence they had never experienced. Roles have changed within a marriage and in less-serious relationships; boyfriends and girlfriends can feel challenged to remain in a committed mindset when faced with the realities of adapting to a military lifestyle. It isn't abnormal to begin asking yourself once facing the last stretch of a deployment if things have changed between the two of you, or if you still feel the same about this person, or most commonly, whether the two of you have grown apart. Try not to feel guilty and understand that this is very normal and common among many people involved in relationships where they are faced with long separations.

I do, however, strongly recommend that you recognize those thoughts and feelings and then place them on hold until your loved one returns home. No one can understand it until you're in the moment and you watch them step off a military aircraft and he or she looks exhausted and proud and so happy to be home, and in that moment any doubt, any concern, any thought that this just isn't going to work out simply vanishes. Most times this is the case, and all things that seemed impossible are suddenly possible and you're able to move forward.

There is another sides of the coin, however, where things are different, no matter how much you wish this were not the case. No matter how hard you try, the two of you just can't regain what was once there. It can't always be happily ever after, but I know that if this is the case in your particular situation, then it is most likely best resolved once they're home. While deployed there are so many demands on each person out there. Distractions can be the difference between life and death, and the most caring thing you can offer people who are already giving so much to a greater good is the absolute best opportunity to focus and complete their mission and come home safe. Everything else should be able to wait until they are home and able to cope on fair ground.

So What Do I Do?

Get ready! There are only ninety days left and so much that can be done. This is such an exciting time. As I mentioned in the beginning of the chapter, it isn't going to be easy, and there will be days when you and your loved one will be riding the emotional roller coaster and there will be days when the days seem endless, but time cannot be stopped, and sooner than you could ever expect they will be coming home.

There are definitely some things you can do in order to prepare for the upcoming change in your life and the big event itself. Some things I recommend are as follows:

1. Start wrapping up some of the individual projects and hobbies you've been working on or at the minimum prepare yourself to possibly put things on hold for a little while when your soldier first gets home.

This applies mostly to romantic relationships. However, mothers and fathers who are welcoming their sons and daughters home, or extended family and friends, should definitely consider allotting some special time to spend with their loved one upon his or her return. It may take a few days to adjust to the sleep patterns after traveling from the other side of the world, but once the soldier has settled in, it's important for those around him or her to readjust their schedules a bit and include some special time for readjustment. This can also be a great time to just decompress and talk about how your soldier is feeling and what it's been like. Don't be surprised, though, if this doesn't happen right away. For many soldiers it can take up to six months before they are able to fully reintegrate with their new environment and able to easily talk about their experiences.

2. Plan the big day! And the next thirty days!

This is a wonderful experience. What an ideal opportunity to plan a way to show someone how much you love them and how much they mean to you. I made a sign for my husband that I planned to hold up for him to see as soon as he found me at the receiving station. It had pictures taped around it of all the major events in our life during the time he was away. This included the birth of our daughter, our other daughter's first day of kindergarten, and some pictures during his R&R visit at home with us. In letters covered in glitter we wrote, "Welcome Home Daddy." It didn't cost much to make, but my whole heart was in the project, and I know that it was something he realized as well.

I also knew the important thing for the first few weeks would be some peace and quiet and time to relax, so I ensured that our calendars were cleared as much as possible and didn't put any pressure on him to go sightseeing or shopping. We really just spent a lot of time at home, talking, relaxing, and enjoying the fact that our family was together again. This is the time to cater to your soldier.

Take his or her needs and interests into account. Be prepared for a lot of sleeping the first week, as he or she begins to adjust to the time change. Remember, most people returning from a deployment are just happy to be home, and the relief to be back is a reward in itself. They are truly enjoying the little things. And finally:

3. Hang in there, stay flexible when the dates change, and stay busy so that time will go quickly.

This isn't going to be easy; the soldier isn't the only one who's anxious. The last three months is normally when loved ones began to feel like enough is enough, but that's when you really have to be strong. Don't give up, don't quit, and most importantly, don't lose sight of what you're really doing this all for. It isn't going to be easy right now, but it will get better, and soon things will change. Soon they will be home.

Journal Entry

1. My soldier will return in three months. Today I feel

_____

_____

_____

_____

_____

_____

2. Time has gone by so slowly today. I can't wait until we can:

_____

_____

_____

_____

_____

_____

_____

3. I will be strong during these last three months because:

_____

_____

_____

_____

_____

Point to Ponder

This is a good time to start reflecting on the deployment and your experiences throughout. Was it harder or easier than you expected it to be? What would you do differently if you could go back and change things? How does this affect the way you will handle the last three months?

Chapter 9

Never Coming Home

But Jesus turned and said to the "Daughters of Jerusalem, don't weep for me, but weep for yourselves and for your children. For the days are coming when they will say, "Fortunate indeed are the women who are childless, the wombs that have not borne a child and the breasts that have never nursed." People will beg the mountains to fall on them and the hills to bury them (Luke 23:28–30).

If you are reading this chapter today and you are faced or are coping with the loss of your loved one, I am so very sorry and I offer my deepest condolences for your loss and for the loss of everyone that loved him or her. This is undoubtedly the most difficult thing you will ever face, and I would be lying if I tried to tell you that it was all going to be okay, because deep down inside, we all know that while only God has the power to heal all hurts, chances are it will never ever be one hundred percent okay again.

My purpose in writing this chapter is because of the realities of today's war on terror and to help offer some understanding and comfort in letting you know that there is no wrong way or right away to handle this. The end state is merely to make it through and continue to be the person your loved one would have wanted you to be. And second, it's a chapter to let you know, as a fellow service member, how much we respect and recognize the tremendous sacrifice that has been made, and the honor of what it all stands for.

A Part of History

As it currently stands, America has lost over forty seven hundred people in the War on Terrorism. These are forty-seven hundred plus families, spouses, children, and loved ones who have had to face the reality that their loved one is never coming home and have come face to face with one of the most difficult experiences of their life.

The loss of life in war is a sacrifice that will never go unrecognized, especially by those who have served with your loved one. There is a deep camaraderie among the military, especially those who have deployed to combat, because of the mutual risk that is shared by them all. The loss of one is more than enough to cause many tears to be shed, many hearts to cry out, and prayers to be spoken on the lips of all who ever came in contact with the fallen person, but one thing that can be agreed upon is that there is no honor greater than the ultimate sacrifice that has been given for the enduring freedoms that we share in this country.

Each person who deploys to war accepts the reality that he or she may very well be placed in harm's way. It is drilled into the hearts and minds of everyone entering the U.S. military that deploying to war is very much a reality, especially in today's global situation, and as those who have chosen to serve, we are required to come face to face with that reality from the beginning.

We begin our military careers training for today's modern battlefield and being pushed to the limit mentally and emotionally in order to develop the level of discipline needed to stand the greatest chance of coming home once deployed. Unfortunately for some, even discipline can't protect them, and we are forced to remember our loved ones as fallen heroes. These men and women are heroes who gave everything in order to defend our freedoms and do their part to provide their families with a better way of life. This is how we should remember our champions. They will forever be a part of the great American history. They are the courageous, the strong, the humble, and those who were willing to do whatever it took to support our great nation in its battle for freedom in a world where our freedoms have been threatened. Consider it a great honor in spite of the pain to have had the chance to love such a brave hero.

There is nothing in the world that can bring your loved one back home now that he or she had given all there is to give, but he or she can always be remembered. Your loved one is now a part of history. It takes a special type of person to willingly accept certain risks for the betterment of the greater good. This may seem ideal in theory; however, these are the people take that theory and make it their reality. This is their life, and they are willing to give everything in order to preserve what they believe in. Sometimes this falls in line with humanitarian efforts, others with deserved peace. Most recently, over forty seven hundred fallen have given their lives for the cause of enduring freedom and the ability to live in a world free from the fear of terrorist activity and a better life for those who have never known real freedom.

I can't begin to say that I understand the depths of pain for those who have lost someone currently serving in the military, but I can say that I thank you. I thank you for encouraging your loved one to fight for what he or she believed in and to hold true to his or her values. I thank you for supporting America's great men and women; in this world you will find no braver. I thank you for helping to nurture and understand another puzzle piece of America's great history and its fight for the enduring freedom of all in this world.

You Are Not Alone

While serving in the army, I was required to undergo the casualty assistance officer training program. One thing I vividly remember is the instructors reiterating to me that there was no higher duty than this. I was to give this mission my complete dedication, for the sheer nature of it required no less. It was emphasized to me that there would be no greater challenge and no deeper meaning than to represent the Secretary of the Army as a member of one of the greatest causes in the world, a representative of the United States military, and a member that had the compassion to not only assist a soldier's next of kin with a most difficult situation but also to represent a symbol of why we continue to risk our lives for this cause.

I remember sitting in my office one afternoon as I watched taped scenarios that I might face serving as a CAO (casualty assistance officer) and five minutes into the video, tears were pouring down my face as I watched the reactions of family members that had to be told their loved one had died while serving in the U.S. military. I realized in that moment that I may not have had the internal strength it would take to walk up to that front door with my dress uniform and look someone in the eye and tell them that their loved one was gone. I was sure that they had chosen the wrong person. I believed that I was much too emotional for such a responsibility. This was until I began to think of my brothers and sisters in arms and their trust in my abilities. As I focused my energy on the brave men and women who would face their fears on the new, modern battlefields that knew no gender, I developed a courage I didn't know I had, and I knew that ultimately I would do whatever it took to be the best I could be with my mission. And I would care for their loved ones as though they were my very own family and honor the fallen in the best way I knew how.

I realize that casualty notification officers, who in actuality are the military officers who will notify you of your soldier's condition, are the last people we pray we ever have to meet, but understand that they are there to honor your loved one and this is never easy for them either. The casualty assistance officer is normally different from the casualty notification officer. The casualty assistance officer is there to support you once you have received the notification that your soldier has passed away. They are there solely to support the family or next of kin of the service member to ensure that they understand all of their entitlements and the processes that relate to this particular issue. The CAO is trained primarily to aid both the next of kin (NOK) and any other assigned beneficiaries as a result of the service member's final requests.

All of this is carefully laid out in various forms and reviewed periodically and immediately prior to a deployment. Everyone is given the opportunity to make any changes as needed to their beneficiary status and percentages of entitlements. It is the responsibility of the CAO to ensure that all parties involved understand the entitlements assigned to them. This may include life insurance, education benefits, and burial benefits. Ultimately the most important thing for me to convey is that these are men and women who are given the responsibility of ensuring that the service member's final wishes are respected. They also ensure that immediate family members understand all of the rights and privileges entitled to them as a result of the most difficult and distressful circumstances.

If you are faced with this horrifying situation, I urge you to allow the military to help you. People are employed solely for the purpose of providing you the counseling you will need in the weeks to come. There are so many different arrangements to be made and so many matters to consider, it is too much to ask of one person who first and foremost has to deal with such a loss. I urge you to let them help. The staff that assists the military in such matters is competent, well trained, and able to answer all your questions and help you in areas you probably haven't even begun to consider. This is their purpose and their own way of honoring the thousands of men and women who have given all there is to give. Allow them the opportunity to make this just a little bit easier for you.

Personal Perspective

I never did have to notify a family about a fallen loved one, but I did serve on the Fort Bliss funeral detail team. My role in this honorable ceremony was to fold and present the flag to the next of kin. I will always hold this as my greatest privilege as a member of the armed forces. It was not an easy task, but one that I accepted with honor and humility. I took a great deal of pride in being the representative who gave families our cherished flag as a token of respect and appreciation for their loved one. There wasn't one funeral that I participated in when during the military ceremony where *Taps* was played and I didn't have to swallow the lump that formed in my throat. I will never forget taking a deep breath before presenting the folded flag to the family and telling them of the nation's gratitude for their loved one's service. I remember staring straight into the eyes of the recipient and speaking with conviction that came straight from my heart.

I want you to know from a very personal perspective, not only mine but from many different officers have I spoken with and have shared the experience of serving as the officers in charge of the military funeral ceremony. We believe in the courage, the passion, and the dedication that it takes to be a military member. Not just anyone can do it and it isn't easy, but when you watch your son or daughter, husband or wife, cousin or best friend transform into one of America's elite, the pride in their uniform speaks volumes. The responsibilities we bear with that uniform are clear, and we opt to put it on everyday anyway. Again, I am so very sorry for the losses that are faced by the families of American military today, but we must always honor their sacrifice by supporting the country they gave their life for.

Where Do I Turn?

It is common for the fallen to leave lonely spouses widowed on a military base, or for parents and extended family to be living in areas far from any military bases and unknown to the military programs that are offered for this situation. At the end of this book, I have attached some helpful numbers and Web sites for families and loved ones to review and contact for more information. The military has numerous programs available for counseling services and detailed support. There are programs both through the armed forces as well as through nonprofit agencies that will offer assistance with the funeral details and memorial services, as well as grief counseling and an explanation of various benefits and entitlements. The most important thing to understand is that there is support available, and no one has to go through any of this scared, confused, or alone.

Don't Turn Away

Oftentimes we believe it's easier to shut everyone out around us in order to cope with our hurts. We trick ourselves into believing we are better off dealing with things alone. Mourning the loss of someone we loved seems best handled as an isolated event, as though somehow the mere fact that getting anyone else involved that didn't even know your loved one the way that you did is a disgrace to their memory.

It's important for all those who are faced with the difficulty of such an abrupt and sudden loss to understand that it is never better alone. Use a support system to help you get through this. The military can handle all of your benefits and entitlements from their end; they will keep you informed and clear on what they need in order to process the entitlements that you are due. There is a well trained and knowledgeable staff that can manage those details, but it's up to you to consider managing your emotional well being.

I sought comfort through my darkest hours at my local church. My church provided me a place where people were joyful, compassionate, and full of love. It was also at church where I was able to allow the Lord's presence surround me with comfort. Even if I simply needed a quiet room to disappear to in order to have some time in private and in prayer, my church gladly obliged. Ultimately, my husband's deployment bore meaning for me as I led myself to church in order to face the hard times and cope with the loneliness. Many loved ones out there are led to bars and nightclubs and find they are emotionally emptier than they were before they left, not to mention the scars this can leave on an intimate relationship between a service member and his or her partner. I highly encourage anyone who is dealing with grief to at least seek some form of assistance or counseling at their local church.

The Bible clearly states in Matthew 18:20: *"For where two or three gather together because they are mine, I am there among them,"* and in grief I would suggest that it is best to be where the Lord is in the midst. Let him comfort you and bring you peace from the deepest areas of your soul.

Journal Entry

** I've decided to leave this journal entry blank. Everyone manages grief differently and will face many different thoughts and emotions. I encourage you to use these lines to describe all that is going through your mind as you finish reading this chapter.

_____

_____

_____

_____

_____

_____

_____

_____

_____

_____

_____

_____

_____

_____

_____

_____

_____

Point to Ponder

Your loved one is a hero and will always be remembered as such. He or she has given all there was to give for the cause of this great country, and although it is an extremely difficult price to pay, this country will be forever thankful for the brave men and women who believed in our nation and represented us with great dignity, honor and strength. America salutes its military and their families.

I am so sorry for your loss.

For Those Left Behind

Chapter 10

Let Us Not Forget the Children

*Therefore, anyone who becomes as humble as
this little child is the greatest in the Kingdom of
Heaven. And anyone who welcomes a little child
like this on my behalf is welcoming me
(Matt. 18:4–5).*

I couldn't finish this book without dedicating a
chapter to our special little angels, the precious
children of our deployed heroes. They are never
necessarily forgotten but often overlooked as these
are the silent sufferers in the family. Children are
resilient. There is no doubt in my mind that they are
able to handle things with an inner strength
unbeknownst to most adults, but they are still
affected when the grownups in their life go away to
war, especially when it's mom or dad. This chapter
is to help us remember the little ones and how to
help them cope with this situation, especially when

they may be the ones trying to help us. God bless them.

Her First Breakdown

It was late at night on a weekday. I was twenty-six weeks pregnant, and my body was aching. My husband had deployed to Iraq one week before. I had just signed finished sending my husband an e-mail and told my four year-old daughter it was time for bed. This was normally a fairly easy task that we went through routinely every night, complete with a bedtime kiss and an "I love you, Mommy."

That night would be different.

My daughter seemed very restless and agitated. I believed her to be overtired and I persisted in telling her that it was time for bed. Two minutes hadn't gone by when all of a sudden she was kicking and screaming, fat tears rolling down her face, as she wailed that she wasn't tired and she wanted her daddy. We spent about thirty minutes that night holding each other as we both agreed that we missed Daddy. I felt utterly helpless against her pain, for I was just barely able to manage my own. At fours years old it was obvious that she was feeling my husband's absence and had become emotionally affected. I realized that as wrapped up as I had become in what I was feeling and in my own hurt, I had taken her feelings for granted.

Methods of Comfort

I was very stung by my daughter's pain that night, and it stayed with me for a long time. She, on the other hand, appeared fine in the morning when she woke up singing songs and asking for breakfast. It was yet another example for me of a child's true resilience and inner strength. Although I knew I couldn't simply move on until the next episode, it was my job as her mom to help her understand what was going on in the small world around her and do whatever I could to make it just a little bit easier. So I began to tell her the story of Daddy in a fairy tale. This was where he was always the hero on the white horse, and she starred as the fairy princess who was waiting for him to slay the dragons and then return to save her from the wicked stepmother. These stories visibly appeared to help her cope with my husband's absence and adjust to the changes in her life and in our daily schedule.

I encourage storytelling. There are times when we can gain deep insight into a child's emotional state by the stories they tell. Other times they may merely want to listen to the story as it is told to them. Story time can also provide some quiet time between you and the child to answer any questions he or she may have about what's going on and help build the bond between you and the child. Although facing a deployment was an extremely difficult challenge for my family, my daughters and I grew very close as a result.

There are other ways to explain to a young child why his or her parent or loved one is gone. This can include a simple conversation, a picture story, or a role-play game. The most important thing is to do what makes your child most comfortable. If your child is a talker, talk to him or her. If he or she is more introverted, try storytelling or a picture story. For the active child I would recommend having a heart to heart conversation during a pause from outdoor play, perhaps an extended water break or ice cream after the game. Adapt to the child and reach his or her level. It will be most rewarding for him or her in the long run and will allow them the greatest opportunity to understand that everything is going to be okay.

When Both Parents Are Deployed

Most people are probably very surprised to know that the military can and will deploy both parents at the same time. I knew many people who couldn't believe I stood the same possibility of being deployed at the same time my husband was deployed regardless of whether we had children. This is one of the sacrifices you must make in order to continue your career as a dual military couple.

The military requires all single parents and dual military couples to keep a family care plan on file in order to serve in the military. The family care plan is documentation that both the service member and the authorized caregiver sign agreeing that if there is to be extended duty or a deployment they are willing to provide care for the child. Oftentimes there are both short and long term care providers and financial support agreements included. This is a way for the military to make it clear that it is the responsibility of the service members to maintain childcare responsibilities in order to support their mission.

As a result more and more children are being left with grandparents, aunts, uncles, and close family friends while both parents are deployed to war or hardship tours overseas. These children are much more susceptible to feelings of abandonment, neglect, anger, and confusion if not properly informed of their circumstances and given a sense of security. It is crucial for children who have both parents deployed, or those who are raised by a single parent who is now deployed, to be reassured that their parent/parents are answering a call of duty and that it's something to be very proud of. The military is now able to offer much more communication between service members and their loved ones through the Internet and phone centers. While this isn't always the case, the chances are pretty high that children will hear from the parents consistently throughout their separation, whether it be through phone calls, e-mails, or letters in the mail.

Making It All Better

For children of all ages there are ways to honor their parents' or loved ones' sacrifice and maintain a positive outlook throughout the challenge of time and distance. Time will naturally move quicker for children as their schedules are often packed with homework, sports, ballet classes, band, and finally bedtime. Before they know it the months will have quickly passed and their family will be reunited once again. Our job as caregivers for these children is to make the most of their distance away from their loved ones by encouraging positive outlets of their experiences.

Age, gender, culture, and background can all play major factors in choosing methods to best relate to the child and strike his or her interest in various projects. By first looking at things from the children's perspective, the chances of success are greater that you will be able to create an opportunity to express their sentiments from their own very personal experience. Remember that it is important for children to understand that their work is not being judged, nor is there any right or wrong way to handle the situation. Every individual is unique, every experience is unique, and the bonds that tie one child to their loved one will be completely distinctive from the bonds that service member maintains with another loved one, so individuality must always be encouraged.

I would like to title these projects, "While You Were Away Gifts." This introduction can lead to many different ideas of projects that kids can do for their beloved deployed person, whether it's Mom and Dad, a big brother or sister, or their favorite uncle or aunt. It all begins with *While You* Were Away I ...

- Made you a photo album
- Wrote you a song
- Drew you these pictures
- Wrote a research paper on the War in Iraq/Afghanistan
- Wrote you a letter every week
- Watched your favorite movie and made you a place setting on the sofa.

The possibilities are endless! Children all over the country can unite together for their loved ones and begin their gifts and projects with the inspiration that *While You Were Away* this was how I wanted to show you how much you were missed. It's a win-win situation and one to touch the hearts of all those who are deployed and join them to the loved ones that are waiting for them to return.

It Won't Always Be Easy

It's easy to forget that kids, adolescents, and teenagers are little people with big feelings, and they are experiencing the world just like anyone else. Deployments are tough, and they are hard for all those involved. There is no exception to being a kid. Some days are going to be tough. Parents, friends, grandparents, caregivers, be ready. It won't always be okay for them. Some days they will feel lonely, frustrated, sad, agitated, or a combination of them all. These are the times they need you the most. Those deployed can't always get to the phone or to the computer, but they have placed their greatest treasure into the hands and hearts of those who are taking care of them, and they are counting on you to help them understand and get through another day.

It's important to encourage children to talk about the hard days. We bear the responsibility of keeping the lines of communication open. Talking through the hard times will be key in coping with such a difficult time. Encourage them to talk about their fears and concerns, their frustrations and anger. This is the first step to healing and acceptance of the deployment. Communication will help to build confidence within our children's hearts that everything possible is being done to bring all of the deployed people home safe and sound. In the end, this confidence is the center of successfully managing the transition of change around them during the absence of their loved one. They will always be thankful when all is said and done that there was always someone there they could talk to, especially if they didn't want to worry those who were away.

Journal Entry

1.   This child favorites hobbies include:

_____

_____

_____

_____

_____

2.   One project we could begin while the child's loved one is away is:

_____

_____

_____

_____

_____

_____

3.   I had a heart to heart with the child today, and he or she shared the following thoughts:

_____

_____

_____

_____

_____

_____

Point to Ponder

The greatest gift we can give to those deployed is the nurture and care of the children they leave behind and those that are in any way affected by their absence. Let us not forget our silent little heroes during this difficult time. They may not always know how to communicate their hurts, but it's our job to figure it out and give them all of the love and protection that they deserve. Let us help our brave men and women focus on their efforts while deployed, as it could be life saving, by providing them with the security that their greatest little gifts are being treated as the precious children that they are. Let us remain patient and understanding when they are angry, positive and reassured when they are afraid, and encouraging and hopeful when they choose to believe for the best.

Chapter 11

Welcome Home—the Readjustment

We can rejoice, too, when we run into problems and trials, for we know that they are good for us – they help us learn to endure. And endurance develops strength of character in us, and character strengthens our confident expectation of salvation (Romans 5:3–4).

None of it was what I thought it would be. None of it. The highs were higher than I could ever have imagined and the lows I had never even anticipated. It started right at first, but quickly the haze began to clear, the euphoria of dreams began to fade, and reality—good, old-fashioned reality—reared its big head and made its way into the picture.

December 1, 2007: Soldiers from the 4th Brigade 1st Cavalry Division began redeploying from Mosul, Iraq. Hesitantly, I flipped the television on and channel surfed until I found the local news. Today I can still feel the lump in my throat that formed as I watched the plane land, the door swing open, and the faces of the anxious families waiting for their loved ones. (I'll never forget those faces.) The soldiers began walking out of the airplane. They marched with the American flag, holding the deepest of respect for all that it stood for. The rest walked with such pride and graciousness, so thankful they were finally on home ground, tired expressions on their faces, smiles they could not suppress. The crowds went wild! Women were screaming, children were jumping up and down, and babies were grasping miniature American flags in their tiny fists. For that moment, for those families, nothing could be more perfect. For the woman standing in her bedroom staring at the TV screen with tears rolling down her face as she watched families welcome their loved ones home, nothing could be more bittersweet.

My husband stepped off the plane and reunited with his family on December 14, 2007. The winds were exceptionally icy that night. My six-year-old daughter and I bore the cold and stood outside, risking hypothermia, hoping only to catch a glimpse of our own personal hero. Unfortunately, in the dark and in the cold we never were able to make out which brave soldier was ours, and we still had to wait for him to turn in his weapon and sensitive equipment before he could be reunited with us.

Approximately forty-five minutes later, a large door opened and a large group of soldiers marched in formation toward their waiting loved ones. It's still amazing to me the level of discipline the military builds inside of oneself that rather than chaotically rush to your family amidst the crowds, after a year of sheer hell and twenty-four-plus hours of travel, soldiers still maintained the discipline to march into that room. They stood in formation and stared at the faces of people who deeply loved them and were eternally grateful for their commitment to freedom. Until finally the magic words were spoken, "4th BDE 1st CAV, dismissed!" And with that they were released … … for the weekend.

Am I Dreaming?

This is magical. Mothers, fathers, husbands, wives, best friends, and siblings—it doesn't matter. This experience is amazing. It's finally over. They made it, they're home. This can be that fresh start everyone needs. The deployment had obviously made an impact on everyone involved and offered fresh perspectives for everyone. Now the question simply becomes what to do with that.

When the soldiers were dismissed I searched frantically for my husband in the crowd. My eyes were scanning the room, physically working to deny the fear in my mind that he hadn't made it, and I walked in one direction praying for our connection to draw us together. Tightly I squeezed my little girl's hand as I gently ignored her question of where was her daddy. I looked and looked until finally, approaching right in front of me with the same look of concern in his eyes that we hadn't made it, was my husband. My daughter and I ran into his arms, wrapped ourselves around him, and thanked God for that moment.

Personally, I had envisioned late nights filled with lots of affection and hours of heart-to-heart talks. I had daydreamed of this moment for many weeks, and all I could picture was endless smiles, passion, and breakfast in bed. The first week was more like my husband and I were on completely different schedules. He would sleep most of the day while I was awake and be up most of the night while I was asleep. I cared enough to allow him this time to recuperate and transition back to living on the other side of the world.

Don't get me wrong, the first week was great. There wasn't anything he could do or say that could possibly steal my joy and gratitude that he was home, not to mention that we were celebrating his birthday two days after his arrival home and Christmas shortly afterward. It was a point in our transition when everything was good. The last fourteen months were finally over. I was happier than I had been in a long time. My ten-month-old daughter was finally going to get an opportunity to get to know her father. My six-year-old was almost as happy as I was and wouldn't leave her daddy's side, and the holidays were approaching. From a physical standpoint my husband came home perfectly healthy. I was in my own happy cloud, but I was being unrealistic and I realized that soon enough.

Reality

This section of my book isn't written to discount the difficulty of what those that were deployed are going through in a transition back home. On the contrary, I'd like to emphasize the exact opposite. There are physical and emotional changes that must occur as a result of re-deployment from a war zone to the home. Because of a lack of knowledge, many times family members don't realize this and they become terribly hurt emotionally because they feel rejected or forgotten. I initially was a victim of my own ignorance. My hopes are that in reading this book loved ones left behind will be able to open their eyes to a different perspective - their loved one's perspective.

It had been five days or so since my husband had come home from Iraq when he requested that I drive him to his unit for some paperwork that needed to be filled out. I don't recall all of the details except that I had to drop him off and return home. At some point in the day he had taken a ride from an acquaintance to the Post Exchange (PX) to do some shopping. Apparently he had called my cell phone a couple of times and I hadn't picked up and he was forced to borrow a ride. Needless to say, when he had finished shopping and was finally able to reach me to pick him up, things were very tense.

I immediately began to panic that so soon after coming home, I had let him down and began racing toward the post to pick him up, as I knew how much this man hated to wait. As luck would have it, I was pulled over on my way to the post and given a speeding ticket and told to slow down. To add to the situation, this had been my second speeding ticket in less than two months (on the same street; you'd think I'd learned my lesson). I arrived to pick him with three strikes against me. I hadn't had my phone with me even though I knew he'd be calling for a ride home, I was pulled over and given a speeding ticket, and it was my second ticket in a short time.

It was all that was needed. You see, there's this overwhelming flood of things going on inside the heart, the mind, and the spirit that most of those who've been deployed aren't even aware of themselves until it's time to release the pressure cooking that's bursting inside of them with pressure.

Needless to say, a mere irritated discussion turned into an outright shouting match in a matter of minutes. I can't help but remember as we were driving home, he was so angry and yelling at me for not admitting that I couldn't drive. I remember listening and trying to understand his side of things, yet realizing that I couldn't get past the thoughts that I felt he had either completely lost his mind in Iraq or had become someone so cruel that his pleasure would come from me admitting weakness and admitting that I was a failure as a driver. It seems silly now, and I realize how wrong we both were that day, but at that time, in that moment, it couldn't be any more serious. See, for me as a woman who had just welcomed her husband home, I had stronger needs than I was willing to admit. I was desperate for his adoration, his approval, and his affection, and the last thing he was prepared to do at that time was tend to my needs, leaving two desperate people -both fighting for one another's love by fighting each other. Its sounds crazy and complicated I know, but for most of us who have been there it all makes perfect sense.

We ended that night with me pacing through the living room, a glass of wine in my hand, screaming at him with tears rolling down my face, he was sitting near the front door on the floor deciding whether he would walk out that night. After fourteen months of lonely nights praying that he would come home and yearning for him, we had managed a couple of days at home before screaming separation at one another ... ahhh young love mixed with transitions from war and changes to the family. Neither one of us could have imagined how much they would impact us. That night we fell asleep holding on to one another so tightly, never wanting to let go.

The Highs and Lows

It wasn't always this way. We didn't spend the entire time fighting. Some moments were very happy. That's just it. The highs were high and the lows were low. It was an emotional roller coaster, and I think there were many factors involved, one being that my husband and I were a young couple. We had only been married four months before he was deployed, and we still had so much to learn about one another. We never sought counseling, and to this day I think that was a big mistake. I consider us to both be very intelligent and educated people, and yet we never had the sense to seek the counseling we needed, and in the end the transition home lasted a lot longer than it probably had to.

If you ask me, I would say that in my opinion it took my husband six months before he was his old self again. Of course, if you ask him, he'd probably say a few weeks - tops. What can I say? It's the nature of the beast. Let me emphasize this—as a result of what has happened to me and what may happen to all that are reading this book and waiting ... *seek counseling!* It's so important to be able to talk to someone. Some sessions can be together; I highly encourage that other sessions be individual, but let someone in with an objective opinion.

When I look back now on all that we endured those first six months he was home, I shake my head in disbelief that I was willing to consider a hundred different terrible options but never the one that would have helped us the most. Ultimately we were lucky, and we made it back together. For others, this isn't the case. Relationships are destroyed, marriages are broken, friendships are killed, and children are left to live in divorced homes because people don't want to realize their need for help. Don't make that mistake; let someone help save your relationship/marriage/friendship.

Recommendation number two: this is the time to enjoy the good times. The sweet moments just don't get any sweeter than they do when there's a homecoming. Mothers and fathers share those special childhood moments that make the soldier miss home. Cook their favorite meal, kiss them goodnight, and bring home a new present. It won't matter it's from the ones that make them feel safest. Friends don't forget that the art of friendship is in the sharing of moments. Friendships are normally built on common interests or the ability to share one's true self with the other. So do that. Be a good talker, be a great listener, and do what the two of you love to do so much together. Just be the kind of friend you would want them to be if you were the one returning home from a place that never quite felt like home. Husbands and wives, for you I offer my deepest words of encouragement. This will not be easy because the needs are mutual. It's a bit easier for parents to forget their own needs when it comes to their children, and for friends to limit their needs when it comes to their friends, but partners just don't get that luxury. We need from them the same way that they need from us, and those two forces can collide and cause fireworks.

Husbands, wives, boyfriends, and girlfriends enjoy the good moments; they are as special as it gets. Study their faces as you watch them sleep; caress their faces and gently rub their cheeks. Listen with your whole heart as you lay their heads in your laps and listen to them talk. Be silent when they don't feel like talking and pray for them that God begins to heal the memories in their minds and the hurt in their hearts. Compliment their bravery and show gratitude for their sacrifice. Think of it as investing for the future, because I guarantee that it will require selflessness from the beginning, but that investment will pay off with a hundred percent return in the future. I have found that there are times in life when it's your time and others when it's not.

In this instance I would request that you let this be their time. Life for them as they know it will never be the same again, and after some time, the clouds will lift, the anger will fade, and it will be your turn. In the meantime, we must look to the Lord to be our comforter, our healer, and the one to meet our inner emotional needs while our partner heals. The Bible says that he will never leave you and never forsake you, and this is the perfect time to put that to the test. I guarantee he'll never lose.

Getting through It with Good Times

About four weeks after my husband's homecoming we took a cruise to the Caribbean. The trip was magical. The transition home hadn't stopped, the adjustments hadn't ceased, but we both agreed that for those seven days we were going to be deliriously happy and enjoy each other the way we had when we first met. And you know what? It worked. To this day I think we still consider that our magical time together. I wouldn't change one single thing about that trip, and we both needed that time to reconnect with one another. And for the rest of our lives that will be one of the sweetest experiences we've ever had together.

Not everyone is in a position to be able to take seven days off and go on a cruise, but the beauty of relationships is that each one is unique and each one has their own special significance. My oldest daughter and I have movie night on Mother's Day. My best friend and I love dressing up and having sushi in pretty restaurants while watching videos of Madonna in concert. My husband and I have fancy dinners. That was always our special treat. I've heard of a couple at church that always shared ice cream night. Whatever it may be, find your bond, enjoy it, and cherish it. Recognize that there is one person in this world who shares that one little thing with you that is unlike anything else with anyone else. These are things that keep service member going every day while fighting wars where they are being shot at, spit on, and considered dispensable, but they sit up late at night and talk amongst one another and share their own versions of your "little special something."

It's Time to Move Forward

I'm writing this chapter a little over a year since my husband's return home, which I believe qualifies me at this point to talk about the gift of moving forward. Some of us will love "career military," and based on the condition of the world today, that simply implies that this deployment may not have been the first nor will it be the last. For others this may be a once-in-a-lifetime experience. Regardless of the situation, the important thing to remember is to never stop moving forward. Heal, learn, love, forgive, and move forward. There is nothing that can change the past, and we have no control over it. Our future, on the other hand, is a different story. We have complete control over how we will handle the future. We can determine what we draw from the past and how we will face our future. It's up to you. This hasn't been an easy time—for some it's been the most difficult thing they've ever been through, but accept that it's over now, even if it's for a short time, and refuse to live in the past. Life will seem so much more meaningful that way. Welcome your loved one home, and good luck to you all!

Journal Entry

1.　　My loved one is arrived home on

_____

2.　　I am having a hard time accepting:

_____

_____

_____

_____

_____

_____

3.　　I want to remember the special things about my loved one. I remember:

_____

_____

_____

_____

_____

_____

_____

4.　　We are struggling right now. Some things to discuss with a counselor and pray about are:

_____
_____
_____
_____
_____
_____
_____
_____
_____

Point to Ponder

What a special part of the story. This is where your loved one finally comes home and their friends and family get to welcome them all back. It isn't going to be all smiles and fairy tales, but the reality is that they are home and at the very least there's a starting point. What becomes of that starting point is ultimately up to you both. This could be the beginning of a new transition or a road to recovery. There will be arguments and there will be frustration and anxiousness, but life is what you make it to be, and my recommendation is that you realize the gift you've been given by being able to welcome them home. For them, the gift is to finally be home. Start your story with gratitude to our Lord and Savior for the strength to get you through it.

Good Luck.

Chapter 12

Spiritual Support

Those who live in the shelter of the Most High will find rest in the shadow of the Almighty. This I declare of the Lord: He alone is my refuge, my place of safety; he is my God, and I am trusting him. For he will rescue you from every trap and protect you from the fatal plague. He will shield you with his wings. He will shelter you with his feathers. His faithful promises are your armor and protection (Ps. 91:1–4).

The Lord says, "I will rescue those who love me. I will protect those who trust in my name. When they call on me, I will answer; I will be with them in trouble. I will rescue them and honor them. I will satisfy them with a long life and give them my salvation"
(Ps. 91:14–16).

Psalm 91 is one of my favorite chapters in the Bible. From the first time I read that chapter I could envision myself underneath the Lord's wings in times of trouble.

Needless to say, I have spent many moments imagining myself seeking peace and tranquility amidst the great challenges in my life. And there have been many.

There's Always a Right Way and a Wrong Way

Regardless of your current spiritual beliefs, one cannot deny the attempt to achieve balance within our universe. In fact, realms of different beliefs from Chinese medicine, to Far Eastern practices have striven to reach or maintain balance between the body, the mind, and the soul. I find this to be further evidence of a Creator of our universe—a Creator based on order—and with order comes harmony and balance. The Bible warns us against excess, and many of us, myself included, have experienced the effects when too much of anything becomes a bad thing.

The laws of balance will apply to decision making and lifestyles as well. There will always be a wrong way and right way, a decision that veers to the right and one that veers to the left. It's inevitable despite how much we like to convince ourselves that there are no wrong choices. I can assure you that there are different consequences for different choices and how those consequences affect us will in turn make us the decision makers as to whether it was wrong for us or right.

When an integral piece of our life is missing, whether it's our child, our spouse, or our best friend, we become faced with choices, temptations, and decisions that will affect not only our current state but also our future state. A huge piece of our life is missing, our daily understanding of what we have become to accept as normal is drastically changing, and there are consequences that are substantially linked with those changes.

Mothers can begin to drink more often because they can't cope with the daily worrying. Fathers may become obsessed with the daily news and stop living their daily lives. Wives and husbands will face temptations from places they never imagined. There is an enemy out there; a spiritual enemy that roams like a "roaring lion seeking to devour." That enemy will use every trick in the book to get you to fail and make your life fall apart around you. Sadly, it all begins with the, "What will it hurt?" theory.

What Will It Hurt?

The unit my husband deployed with was called the 4th BDE 1st Cav. Many people back on our post referred to the female spouses as the "4-1 wives" while their soldiers were deployed. They had earned a special nickname because of the decisions some of them had chosen to make while their husbands were away. Unfortunately, many of them grouped together and began dressing up, going to bars, dancing at nightclubs, and causing all sorts of trouble, including intimate relationships with other men. Some of these men were even close friends of their husbands, friends that had been entrusted to respect the bonds of marriage and instead abused a delicate situation and destroyed the families of friends they once cared about.

I am not even beginning to assume that all wives faced with many months alone will make these same decisions, but I am admitting that it is common. Women begin to find themselves weighed down with the demands of the household, work, children, school, family, or the day-to-day occurrences that they are now forced to face alone. There are times when they may go months without hearing from their spouses, and the pressure is unimaginable. Regardless of whether or not they go on living their daily lives, there's a nagging concern that never stops. And the emptiness of your partner's absence is very hard to fill.

So what may begin as an innocent, good-natured night out to release some stress turns into a face-to-face encounter with their loneliness and vulnerability. If a little bit of alcohol is added to the mix, the pressures seem to double in a matter of minutes, and the vulnerabilities deepen, and now there is a door left wide open in her life, a door that the enemy will use to tempt and destroy. At this moment up strolls Mr. Handsome with some sweet talk and bad intentions, and what may seem to be a "harmless" situation turns into a very big mistake.

Husbands who are left behind are just as vulnerable. Most times when husbands are left behind they are consistently encouraged by their friends to "man up" and stop acting like a sissy. They are taunted with accusations of "acting like a girl" by honoring the Lord and their family and remaining faithful to their loved ones. They are taunted by their own pride, tempted by their own physical needs. This is a tragedy, but it is the truth. The enemy is out there willing to use anyone to destroy the Lord's perfect creation—the bonds of husband and wife and the beauty of the family.

I want to encourage everyone reading this that it does not have to be this way. I want to enforce the idea that there are other solutions to this loneliness and that when we are placed in the positions (and I promise they will come), and we begin to think to ourselves, "What will it hurt?" I can assure you that there is only one answer to that: it will hurt everyone you love, especially the ones you would probably never want to hurt in your life. See, it just so happens that things done in darkness have a way of being brought into the light, whether it's a result of an unexpected pregnancy, an incurable sexually transmitted disease, or a close family friend who sees you leaving somewhere you should never have been. Injustices have a way of coming back again and again and rearing their ugly heads, and that's no way to live. There is another answer.

Temptation is real, and it is not selective to the bad people. On the contrary, it pays a visit to every single human being roaming the planet. There is nothing wrong with being faced with temptation. It happens, but we are given tools and the strength to fight. God does not leave us unarmed in these spiritual battles. In Ephesians 6:11–17 (NLT), Paul talks about putting on the whole armor of God. In the scriptures he states:

> *Put on all of God's armor so that you will be able to stand firm against all strategies and tricks of the Devil. For we are not fighting against people made of flesh and blood, but against the evil rulers and authorities of the unseen world, and against wicked spirits in the heavenly realms. Use every piece of God's armor to resist the enemy in the time of evil, so that after the battle you will be standing firm. Stand your ground, putting on the sturdy belt of truth and the body armor of God's righteousness. For shoes, put on the peace that comes from the Good News, so that you will be fully prepared. In every*

battle you will need faith as your shield to stop the fiery arrows aimed at you by Satan. Put on salvation as your helmet, and take the sword of the Spirit, which is the word of God. Pray at all times and on every occasion in the power of the Holy Spirit. Stay alert and be persistent in your prayers for all Christians everywhere.

As a soldier, I have really enjoyed this scripture and have found that the Lord has drawn me to it at least two times in my life when I really found myself under a strong spiritual attack. The truth is simple: there is a war in the spiritual realm, a war of souls, and as God's children we are not immune to these battles, but we are protected. I speak this truth from my own living experience. I endured the tests, trials, and temptations of being left alone for fourteen months while my husband was away. I thank God that I am able to look back now and be proud of that fact that through his strength, support, and wisdom, I honored myself and my family.

When I read the scripture about the armor of God I think about protecting my belly or my "gut instinct" with the truth and not Satan's lies. I put on my body armor or my "whole being" with his righteousness, knowing that I am fully covered and protected in my father's righteousness. For shoes I put on peace. In other words, I literally strive to walk in the peace of the Lord's protection and in knowing that he is on my side. I proudly hold up my shield of faith. The scripture says in every battle, not some, not most, but in *every* battle we will need faith. Faith protects us from the arrows (a.k.a., the bad news, the discouragement, the pain, the temptations, the lusts, the sorrows, etc.) that Satan aims at us. Faith says we believe that we are victorious and blessed and will get through this experience stronger than ever. Put on salvation as your helmet. In other words, protect your mind through salvation. Don't fill your mind with garbage, whether it's bad thoughts of distress, negative news on TV, or lustful movies or books. Protect your mind and guard your heart. And finally take the sword of the Spirit, the word of God. Your sword is your weapon. So fight and fight hard, but ensure that your weapon of choice is the knowledge of the word of God. Fight the battles by reading the word, letting the word move inside you, and speaking that word from your lips. This is how we prepare for battle. This is our armor that will guarantee us a victory. And as a soldier reaching out to thousands of people who love their soldiers, I encourage you to fight to win!

Vulnerability

If I think back from October 2006 until December 2007 and strive for the word that best described me during that time, I would have to use the word *vulnerable*. In fact, it was probably the period of my life where I have faced one of my greatest vulnerabilities. I was pregnant, I was new to the life of the military, I was in a new marriage, and I was in a new job with brand-new responsibilities. I was truly vulnerable. And like anyone else, I was faced with many decisions.

The temptations and the attacks on my life were ever prevalent, but like his promise, the quiet call of the Lord was also there, and my heart could not turn away. I was not called to enter into some deep, ritualistic religion. I don't discourage anyone from entering the Lord's house for any reason, but in my own particular life I needed a relationship, not a religion. And so I utilized that time to begin building that relationship.

Rather than have my baby and head off to the parties and nightclubs, I began attending an amazing local church. I found a support system I never knew existed. I met good people who genuinely cared about my wellbeing and family's welfare. I found people whose shoulder's I could cry on when it just got too hard and I felt completely alone. I found people that would comfort me, join me in prayer, and help me to leave the service recharged and ready to face the world again.

I realize that there are many forms of believing out there, and I have a true respect for everyone's individual decision, but I had to include this chapter to highlight the key, the real reason I was able to make it through such a difficult time successfully. It wasn't because of some supernatural internal strength, or easier circumstances. On the contrary, I'd even venture to say I had it pretty hard, but I turned to the Lord for support and to his house for protection, and I was never once let down. In the end, this relationship actually helped create a greater sense of purpose for me in relation to my husband's deployment. It helped me use our time apart to become wiser and softer and spiritually sound. It also helped me to fill my husband with encouragement and good news and the faith that the Lord was protecting him and touching our lives. For the ones who are spending day after day in combat, good news and encouragement can be a well of water to a thirsty soul.

It's Not Too Late

Loved ones reading this chapter may feel it's come too late. Mistakes have already been made. Weakness won out in a certain circumstance, and now you're riddled with guilt. For others, parents, siblings, and friends, you've made decisions since your loved one's departure that you feel now have you tangled in ropes. The drinking has gotten out of hand, or you can't stop worrying and obsessing over every action occurring in the Middle East. For others vices are getting the best of you. Wives and children are eating themselves into obesity, endangering not only their health but also their self-esteem. Husbands are smoking themselves straight to lung cancer, and siblings are driving at unhealthy speeds or taking crazy chances on their motorcycles. Actions and behaviors you would normally never do are now commonplace since having to cope with a loved one who is deployed. It feels like you're drowning so far under you can't see the light outside anymore.

I am here to tell you that it is not too late. It is never too late to choose to change things and start over. Our Lord and Savior will never leave us nor forsake us. That is his promise. And among all the gambles so many are willing to take, I would put my money on a promise from the Lord. His forgiveness is eternal, and his desire to comfort you will never fade. I am living proof. I have never been a saint, nor did I deserve any special treatment, but when I turned to him, he accepted me just as I was and forgave all my sins, my bad decisions, my poor judgment, and my weaknesses and made me feel brand new.

There is no shame in the Lord. All it takes is a choice, and the nice thing is that the choice is always yours to make. You can ask for forgiveness and he will *always* give it. You can ask for his presence, and he will be right there. You can ask for him to come into your life and fill the loneliness and the angels will celebrate! And from that point on, when faced with the temptations, the tough times, the weak moments, the arguments, the days when you want to throw a glass against the wall just to hear it break, he is there to make you stronger and peaceful. He is there to whisper in a soft voice and speak to your heart and offer you encouragement and understanding. He was there for me through every difficult moment, and I quickly stopped feeling so alone.

In Him

I can only hope that throughout this book there have been areas that have helped readers understand their service member's situation and their own in a different light. I hope that through my own experience and through the experiences of others that contributed to this book people are able to see that they are not alone in their struggle.

Maintaining spiritual support from my local church and the reading of my Bible was the backbone of success for me. It kept my eyes focused on the right things, my heart filled with patience and love, my mind open to understanding, and my feet walking forward and not looking back. My faith was challenged at times, but I had warriors all around me to help fight the battles I could not fight alone, and I am eternally grateful. My final words of encouragement for the spiritual support is to find a way for God to touch your heart and your life so that he can carry you through this difficult but temporary time, and I guarantee you will never regret it.

The Military Member

I want you all to know that there is no easy answer as to how to manage the realities of the profession your service member has chosen. It is not easy, but nothing good ever is. We simply have to see the honor and dignity that comes with such a brave choice. It takes a very special kind of person to raise his or her right hand and give up a selfish sense of existence. I have had the great satisfaction of staring into the hearts of hundreds of military who have deployed in our fight for freedom or been willing to do so and listened to their stories. I have heard the compassion in their hearts and seen the weight of all they have borne from the look in their eyes, and all I can say is thank you. I am so thankful that our country is full of so many amazing, selfless, and dedicated men and women who have given so much for something so much bigger then themselves. I am so thankful that I was given the pleasure of being able to serve beside these men and women and to now give back to them by helping to serve the families and the friends who love them. God bless America and its protectors.

Journal Entry

1. I am being faced with temptations in my life. Some effects of making the wrong choice are:

_____

_____

_____

_____

2. My loved one would feel _____ and would say to me

_____

_____

_____

_____

3. My current relationship with the Lord is

_____

_____

_____

_____

I want to improve this relationship by:

_____

_____

_____

_____

_____

4. Lord, I pray to you. Please forgive me
for:_____

_____

_____

_____

_____

And help me to start over again.

Point to Ponder

If you are facing the deployment of someone
you love or care for, then it is your duty to support
him or her as much as possible. Your loved one's
greatest support is in knowing that you are honoring
him or her by taking care of yourself physically,
emotionally, and spiritually. If they know you are
okay, than they are able to focus on the mission and
tasks at hand, which in turn can be the kind of focus
that saves their life or the lives of others. Set
yourself up for success through this very
challenging time. Search for a greater power than
your own to provide you with the strength, peace,
and comfort that will lead your steps to
righteousness and honor of your loved one.
Remember that the Lord will *never* leave you nor
forsake. You are his precious child.

For Those Left Behind

Appendix

Scriptures & Passages That Help

I wanted to include some scriptures to read and meditate on for the difficult times we will face during a deployment. I hope that they bless you as they have blessed me.

First Time You Get the News
Victory and strength

Judges 4–7: These are the stories of Deborah and Gideon, strong strategic and wartime thinkers who were victorious in battle.

Isaiah 50:7–9: Because the Sovereign Lord helps me, I will not be dismayed. Therefore, I have set my face like a stone, determined to do his will. And I know that I will triumph. He who gives me justice is near. Who will dare to oppose me now? Where are my enemies? Let them appear! See, the Sovereign Lord is on my side! Who will declare me guilty? All my enemies will be destroyed like old clothes that have been eaten by moths!

The First Week Your Loved One Is Deployed
Coping with grief and finding
strength in the Lord

Genesis 39–41: The story of Joseph in Potiphar's house, his imprisonment, and his delivery to Ruler of Egypt. This is the story of God's good purpose realizing itself through the hard times.

Matthew 26:38: He told them, "My soul is crushed with grief to the point of death. Stay here and watch with me." He went on a little farther and fell face down on the ground, praying, "My father! If it is possible, let this cup of suffering be taken away from me. Yet I want your will, not mine."

Through the Misunderstandings
Finding peace and tranquility
through the tension

Acts 12: The story of Paul's imprisonment. The special thing about this chapter is that despite the murder of James and his own imprisonment, Paul was able to find peace. In fact, the Bible states that when an angel of the Lord helped Paul escape from prison, he was asleep! He was asleep the night before he was to be placed on trial! Most of us upon facing a trial where we could assume the deadliest of outcomes would not be able to find the kind of peace that comes only through faith and sleep. Th ink about Paul's faith and the Lord's recognition of that faith by saving his life through a mighty miracle.

Colossians 1:11–12: We also pray that you will be strengthened with his glorious power so that you will have all the *patience* and *endurance* you need. May you be *filled with joy* always thanking the Father, who has enabled you to share the inheritance that belongs to God's holy people, who live in the light.

Prayers for the Newborn Baby
Prayers for the Lord's precious gift

1 Samuel 1: This is the story of Hannah's prayers to the Lord to give her a son. She wanted a child so badly that she was willing to bear the child and then give him as a gift to the Lord by having him grow up within the church. This child was such a great gift to his mother from the Lord that she showed her appreciation by dedicating him to our heavenly Father.

Jeremiah 1:5: I knew you before I formed you in your mother's womb. Before you were born I set you apart and appointed you as my spokesman in the world.

Encouragement and Strength
When We Are Weary

We all need some uplifting and encouragement when it seems like it'll never end and time is moving so slowly.

Genesis 29: This is one of the Bible's great stories of patience. This is the story of Jacob's determination to marry the woman he loved. It took Jacob not only seven years of waiting for his bride but also of hard labor for her father. It also required him to dedicate an additional seven years of hard work. I can safely assume that there were times Jacob was probably weary and frustrated, maybe even times he wanted to give up, but when the seven years were over the Bible says his love was so great that years then seemed like minutes.

Isaiah 40:30–31: Even youths will become exhausted, and young men will give up. But those who wait on the Lord will find new strength. They will fl y high on wings like eagles. They will run and not grow weary. The will walk and not faint.

When Our Hearts Are Heavy with Concern

When we haven't heard from our loved ones and we
believe for their safety

1 Chronicles 14: David was a great warrior and a
proud soldier. He was given the Lord's divine favor
and was a conqueror in many battles. This chapter
of the Bible discusses David's victory against the
Philistines. David asked the Lord if he would give
him victory, and the Lord replied, "Yes, go ahead. I
will give you the victory." This is an encouraging
story to read for yourself and for your soldier.

Philippians 4:6–7: Don't worry about anything;
instead, pray about everything. Tell God what you
need, and thank him for all he has done. If you do
this, you will experience God's peace which is far
more wonderful than the human mind can
understand. His peace will guard your hearts and
minds as you live in Christ Jesus.

**When the Service Member Loses One of Their
Own**

Help to reach out and pray for their continued
strength and mental toughness.

&

Losing Your Loved One

Beginning the road to acceptance and healing

Psalm 13: This special psalm touches the hearts of many because of David's distress and call on God. It is a good example that life isn't always fair, and we live in a fallen world. However, we are given the choice to manage our sorrows by setting our sights on our heavenly Father and put our trust in his unfailing love.

Psalm 6:4–7: Return, O Lord, and rescue me. Save me because of your unfailing love. For in death, who remembers you? Who can praise you from the grave? I am worn out from sobbing. Every night tears drench my bed; my pillow is wet from weeping. My vision is burred y grief; my eyes are worn out because of all my enemies.

Peace During R&R
Make this a special and memorable time

Esther 5: I think this story is very fitting because it talks about the things Esther did in order to prepare some time with her husband and find favor with him. As a result of her careful preparation and care, the king offered her anything she wanted. This is a good example of how we should prepare our homes and hearts for our loved ones redeploying home after being so very far away. Let's keep a mentality of servitude and serve one another and enjoy the rewards when our soldiers realize all that has been done for them.

John 14:27: I am leaving you with a gift—peace of mind and heart. And the peace I give isn't like the peace the world gives. Do don't be troubled or afraid.

Preparation for Redeployment

Requesting the Lord's divine action in
your relationship with your soldier.

Genesis 24: This is the story of the coming together of Isaac and Rebekah. Isaac was operating under his father's promise from God that he would be blessed. In reading the story, it is clear that Rebekah was God's chosen mate for Isaac. As a result, there was instant clarity on her part that she was to return to meet her future husband without delay, and Isaac immediately fell in love with her.

Ultimately we must understand that our heavenly Father does not make mistakes, and his promises are true. When we allow for his divine action we can assure ourselves that the result will be good. I encourage everyone to read this story and remember that the Lord wants us to be blessed and to be fulfilled with the loved ones in our life. His work is good and we must turn to this truth when things begin to get challenging or stressful as we prepare to reunite with our soldiers.

1 Corinthians 13:4–7: Love is patient and kind. Love is not jealous or boastful or proud or rude. Love does not demand its own way. Love is not irritable, and it keeps no record of when it has been wronged. It is never glad about injustice but rejoices whenever truth wins out. Love never gives up, never loses faith, is always hopeful, and endures through every circumstance.

1 Corinthians 13:13: There are three things that will endure—faith, hope, and love—and the greatest of these is love.

Fighting the Battle of Discord—the First thirty Days at Home
Battling strife, anger, and hostility. Focusing on love, patience, serving, and humility

Timothy 2:23-26: Again I say, don't get involved in foolish, ignorant arguments that only start fights. The Lord's servants must not quarrel but must be kind to everyone. They must be able to teach effectively and be patient with difficult people. They should gently teach those who oppose the truth. Perhaps God will change those people's hearts, and they will believe the truth. Then they will come to their senses and escape from the Devil's trap. For they have been held captive by him to do whatever he wants.

Hosea 2:19: I will make you my wife forever, showing you righteousness and justice, unfailing love and compassion.

1 Peter 3:1–2: In the same way, you wives must accept the authority of your husbands, even those who refuse to accept the Good News. Your godly lives will speak to them better than any words. They will be won over by watching your pure, godly behavior.

Proverbs 23:22–25: Listen to your father, who gave you life, and don't despise your mother's experience when she is old. Get the truth and don't ever sell it; also get wisdom, discipline, and discernment. The father of godly children has cause for joy. What a pleasure it is to have wise children. So give your parent's joy! May she who gave you birth be happy.

46597124R00122

Made in the USA
San Bernardino, CA
10 March 2017